The Hidden Reality Surrounding the Environment of the Crucifixion of Jesus Christ

Agustín Pimentel

ARPress
ILLUMINATING IDEAS
EMPOWERING VOICES

ARPress
45 Dan Road Suite 5
Canton MA 02021

Hotline: 1(888) 821-0229
Fax: 1(508) 545-7580

Ordering Information:
Quantity sales. Special discounts are available on quantity purchases by corporations, associations, and others. For details, contact the publisher at the address above.

Printed in the United States of America.

ISBN-13:	Softcover	979-8-89389-635-0
	eBook	979-8-89389-636-7

Library of Congress Control Number: 2024921881

CONTENTS

Preface..5

Acknowledgments 7

Introduction..11

Chapter 1: A Defeated Enemy...15

Chapter 2: Bad Decisions Have Bad Consequences.............18

Chapter 3: Our Problem-Focused Society 20

Chapter 4: The Voluntary Substitute...................................23

Chapter 5: But When the Fullness of Time Was Come..........27

Chapter 6: The Seventy Weeks of Daniel 32

Chapter 7: Uncertain Birth of Jesus....................................34

Chapter 8: What Was the Origin of Christmas? 40

Chapter 9: Is the Date of Jesus's Birth Wrong?...................45

Chapter 10: Nimrod's Appearance.......................................49

Chapter 11: Nimrod's Aberrant Sin.....................................53

Chapter 12: The True Origin of Christmas 56

Chapter 13: Who Carried the Cross That Was Used to
            Crucify Christ, Jesus, or Simon of Cyrene?..............59

Chapter 14: Know the Truth Outside of Roman Myths 66

Chapter 15: Apparent Contradiction....................................70

Chapter 16: The True Day and Time Christ Died.................73

Chapter 17: Relation of the Time of Passover to the
            Death of Christ 79

Chapter 18: Bought at the Price of Blood............................82

Chapter 19: Appropriate Satisfaction...................................98

Chapter 20: The Cross as a Religious Symbol......................104

Chapter 21: Symbol of Shame and Curses.................................108
Chapter 22: What Happened to the Nails That Were
            Used to Crucify Christ?...111
Chapter 23: New Year's Celebration 114
Chapter 24: The Second Coming of Christ.............................115
Chapter 25: Debt Settled 119
Chapter 26: Characteristics of the Human Being 124
Conclusion...133
Etymology..137

PREFACE

It is still very regrettable that there are many people who have not been able to comprehend the reality of God's plan for humanity, which is established even before the foundation of the world. But also, at this point in life, many have not managed to understand the reason for death and the suffering we face during our pilgrimage on the earth. We believe that this happens because we do not have sufficient knowledge of what the Bible teaches us, which leads us, due to lack of biblical answers, many times, to doubt the existence of God. Without realizing it, we enter into the traps of the enemy, resulting in the loss of the faith and hope that we must have in the Lord, and thus come to place all responsibility and control of destiny in the hands of man (Revelation 19–22; Romans 5, 3–5).

That is not what the Bible teaches us because God controls and determines and has a plan for everything that happens around the globe. Nothing gets out of his hands or his control. If we are unable to believe that, then, without a doubt, we find ourselves with enough reason to become frustrated and live without any hope. There are many realities that are not within the reach of our understanding—realities that are hidden—which, once knowing them, can cause a profound change in our lives. We hope that you will accompany us through this meticulous journey where we will be presenting hidden truths that, despite the fact that we often have them in front of us, we perhaps have not paid them the necessary attention to be able to fully understand them.

An example of one of these hidden realities is the one that we have selected to delve into all its surroundings. This will be a challenge for us because, at the end of this work, many will possibly come to a negative position or positive acceptance, but who knows? Many, for not concentrating enough from the start or that perhaps what we present here is not of great interest to them, may come to disagree with us.

But of this, we are very sure: we will be breaking down barriers of disbelief and divulging mysteries that will be challenging the scope of your understandings. We believe that the topic "The Hidden Reality Surrounding the Environment of the Crucifixion of Jesus Christ" will be a challenge to take it to an ample level of undeniable reality; although for many, it may be controversial. Pay attention. These things are what God wants you to discover this time.

As we have already hinted, we will be touching on many points in relation to the environment of the crucifixion, such as the true details of the cross; details of the nails used to crucify Christ; details of the exact day that Jesus Christ died; what are the gallows; details of what involved dying on a cross; and something that cannot be lost, which will be a controversial issue, which is from where Christ carried the cross and how many times he fell carrying it. In short, there are many existing unknowns and questions that we will try to clarify with the help of the Holy Spirit.

ACKNOWLEDGMENTS

It was finally achieved. And now it remains for me to give the most expressive thanks to the Lord for this opportunity he has given me to write this book, which is born from my thesis prepared for Dayspring Theological University and thus fulfill the requirement for the course of the doctoral specialty, PhD, which has been another wish also within my proposed achievements to carry out. Thank you, Lord. Thank you so much.

Now I want to continue thanking all those in my family who have been with me, supporting me so that I could finish this very important book. I am also grateful for all those who have been giving me strength and encouragement so that I continue with a great desire to elaborate this book in a constructive way. Thanks to God. I return and let you know that I am very happy because I can continue to count on people around me who really love me and appreciate me. Thank you very much.

I greatly appreciate each prayer and the much-needed support of my people who were there in the moments that I needed them and asked for their help. In short, to all those who, in one way or another, have been present. Again, thanks to the members of the church of the Agua de Vida Evangelistic Movement in Philadelphia, which I am honored to pastor, and to the associate pastor Carmen María Ramírez for being my right hand and who is always present to help me without any condition or interest demanded not only in the ministry of the church but also in the ministry of the movement, which, thanks to God, I preside over.

I also continue to give the most expressive thanks to Sister Wanda Margaret Lluveras, who, as I have already expressed myself about her, helped me not only in matters of music but also in the corrections of my written works.

As I have indicated previously, God used her so that I could get to know the university, where the doors were opened for me so that I could study and achieve these precious achievements. It was through her that I received the blessing of connecting with the University of Dayspring and that they give me the opportunity to study, teach university classes, and achieve the achievements of a master's degree in theology and a doctorate in theology as well as this specialty doctorate in theology (PhD) regardless of my blind condition. I cannot stop repeating these words, and I will always keep repeating this: at some point in our lives, there have been people who make our lives easier to carry, either because of their company, their work, their advice, or their so appreciable genuine affections.

May God bless these important people in our lives. Among them, I can only mention a few because it would be impossible for me to mention all those who have helped me fulfill my expectations: José de Jesús and his wife, Ruth (José de Jesús made the final and exhaustive edit of this book.); my friend and brother Harry Aponte; all my fellow students who have been with me arm in arm during class periods; Héctor Lugo; my friend Freddy González; and Milagros Acosta and her husband, José Muñoz. I do not want to fail to mention Dr. Ada Vidal and her husband, Dr. Víctor Vidal, who have also selflessly given me their help. Dr. V. Vidal volunteered to provide a final review to this English translation. And I want to express my gratitude to Dr. Ada Vidal for creating the entire montage for the cover photo as well as to Pastor Isaias Perales for taking the cover photograph.

Many thanks to Dr. Adrián Nájera, PhD, president of the Dayspring Theological University, who has also given me his unconditional support. And I cannot fail to mention that, at my graduation from Master of Theology course, I presented myself in this way, joking and saying these words: "I present to you the doctor and almost Dad, Minister Agustín Pimentel. What will he be calling me after this?"

Also, thanks to our chancellor Dr. Fernando Quiles Moreno, PhD, to whom I owe a lot of respect. And I thank him very much for his support and encouragement so that I could move on. He has also been a good adviser, and I repeat that, on some occasions, he has also called me Punta De Lanza (I repeat again; ask him why).

I cannot fail to mention Minister Jose Hernández, his son Dany, and his nephew Denis Hernández, who are members of our church and who were in charge of photographing me for the biography photo of this book. Thanks, guys. I hope you have achieved a miracle with my portraits.

Nor can I forget to thank my son Agustín Pimentel Jr. for his much-appreciated help with this book. Thank you, macho. I also thank one of my sons, George Correa, because he has always been at my disposal as far as art is concerned.

Once again, my deepest thanks to God, and from my heart to all those mentioned above, I will be eternally grateful for everything.

Lastly, my appreciation to Dr. Victor Vidal for taking the time to review the translation of this book from Spanish to English.

INTRODUCTION

There are many people around the world who scrupulously and without any qualms dare to say and even somewhat allege that the Bible has been contaminated through alterations, editions, or revisions. But it is good that you know, in case you did not know, that the books of the Old Testament were written approximately from 1400 to 400 BC, while the books of the New Testament were written approximately from 40 to 90 DC. So it has been almost between 1,900 and 3,400 years since a book of the Bible was written. Currently, the original manuscripts have possibly been lost, and it is very likely that they no longer exist. It is also very true that, during this time, the books of the Bible have been copied countless times.

Despite all of this, we can still trust the Bible. Yes, we can trust the Bible because when God began to inspire man to write his word, it was inspired by God through the Holy Spirit. Let's read 2 Timothy 3, 16–17 and John 17:17. You will notice that no part of the Bible applies to whether or not copies were made out of the original manuscripts.

Despite how meticulous and strict the scribes were with the replication of the scriptures, we can say that possibly one or the other could have been perfect. It is true that small differences may have arisen in the various copies of the Scriptures as a result. Of all the thousands of Greek and Hebrew manuscripts in existence, no two were identical. That is until the printing press was finally invented in AD 1500. However, any scholar or Bible scholar interested in the documents will agree that the Bible has been remarkably preserved through the centuries. Many copies of the Bible dated to the fourteenth century BC are almost identical to the contents of the third century BC copies.

Something that is very surprising is that when the Dead Sea scrolls were discovered, the scholars were amazed to see the similarity they had with other ancient copies of the Old Testament, although the Dead Sea scrolls were hundreds of years older than any of those previously discovered. Even many skeptics and critics of the Bible admitted that the Bible has been transmitted over the centuries much more accurately than any other document or book no matter how old.

Currently, at least until now, there is absolutely no evidence that the Bible has been revised, edited, or altered in any systematic way. The large number of biblical manuscripts makes it easy to recognize any attempt to distort the Word of God. There is no major doctrine of the Bible that is questioned as a result of minor differences between the manuscripts. Therefore, there is no reason to doubt the Holy Scriptures (the Bible). God has preserved his word despite the unintentional mistakes and intentional attacks by human beings.

We can be absolutely confident that the Bible we have today is the same Bible that was originally written. The Bible is the word of God, and we can trust it (2 Timothy 3:16; Matthew 5:18). We hope you keep in mind that we, true believers in Christ, must always be learning and must never stop delighting in it because it makes us grow in knowledge and wisdom. God speaks to those who take care to listen attentively to him, whether by reading, meditating, and studying Scripture. The Bible is very essential for growth, more than decisive for real changes and decisive for maturity.

"Forever, oh Jehovah, your word stands in heaven" (Psalm 119:89). The discovery of the Dead Sea scrolls in 1947 has been called the largest archaeological find of the twentieth century. The manuscripts hidden in the caves near Qumran are the oldest known copies of the key books of the Old Testament. In 2007, the San Diego Natural History Museum hosted an exhibition of twenty-four of these rolls. One topic often repeated in the exhibition was that, for the past two thousand years, the text of the Hebrew Bible (the Christian Old Testament) remained virtually unchanged.

Followers of Christ who believe that the Bible is the eternal and unchanging word of God consider this extraordinary preservation to be no mere coincidence. The psalmist wrote, "Forever, Oh Jehovah, your word stands in heaven. From generation to generation is your faithfulness" (Psalm 119:89–90). Jesus said, "Heaven and earth shall pass away, but my words shall not pass away" (Matthew 24:35).

The Bible is more than a historical relic. It is the living and powerful word of God (Hebrews 4:12), where we meet the Lord and discover how to live for him and honor him. "I will never forget your precepts, for by them you have preserved my life" (Psalms 119:93).

CHAPTER 1

A DEFEATED ENEMY

Satan was an angel created by God, who turned against him (Isaiah 14:13) and became the leader of a kingdom of evil spirits called demons, which are his "angels" (Matthew 25:41). His power is great, both in the celestial kingdom and on earth, and should not be underestimated. However, while Satan and his forces are fearsome enemies, Jesus Christ has crushed the power of Satan, fulfilling the prophecy of Genesis 3:15. The cross of Christ secured the victory (John 12:31). "He of this world has already been judged" (John 16:11). And one day, Jesus will completely destroy the power of Satan and purify creation (2 Peter 3:10).

The power of Satan in the heavenly realm/spirit world

Satan's power has a reputation in the spiritual realm (Jude 1:9), where it has limited access to God's presence (Job 1:6). The book of Job offers insight into the relationship between God and Satan. In Job 1:6–12, Satan appears before God and reports that he has been "going about the earth and walking in it" (verse 7). God asks Satan if he has considered his servant Job, and Satan immediately accuses Job of falsehood, saying that he only loves God for the blessings he gives him. Satan says, "Now stretch out your hand, and touch everything he has, and you will see if he does not blaspheme against you in your very presence" (verse 11).

God grants Satan permission to touch Job's possessions and family, but not his life, and Satan left God's presence. In Job 2, Satan comes back into God's presence, and this time, he is allowed to affect Job's health. (The rest of the book is from Job's perspective, providing an example on how to deal with suffering.) This is an important passage because it shows Satan's position in the spiritual realm. He is able to accuse the people in the very presence of God, and Jude 1:9 shows that even the archangel Michael needs the help of the Lord to defeat the devil. However, Satan is obviously prevented from spreading all his wrath. He is still a being below God, and his power is limited.

Satan's power on earth

Job 1 also reveals that Satan spreads evil and causes direct harm on earth. His best-known and most important action on earth occurred in the garden of Eden. Genesis 3 speaks of Satan's temptation of Eve, "mother of all the living," (verse 20) and then of the first sin. This act, along with that of Adam, the husband of Eve, is what introduced sin to the world, and therefore, all mankind must be redeemed from sin in order to be with God.

"One day Jesus found a woman who had been crippled by an evil spirit for eighteen years" (Luke 13:11). Jesus attributes the disease to Satan, who had kept her "bound" (verse 16). Satan's power is real but was easily defeated by our Lord: "And he laid his hands on her; and she immediately straightened up, and glorified God" (verse 13). The miracle of Jesus was a clear demonstration of his authority over Satan. Since his incitement of evil on earth, Satan has been called the "prince," "god," or "ruler," of this world (John 14:30, 12:31, 16:11; 2 Corinthians 4:3–4; Ephesians 2:2; Colossians 1:13). He is the enemy of God and the truth (Matthew 13:24–30; 2 Thessalonians 2:9–12), and he does whatever he can to tempt people (Genesis 3; Luke 22:31; 1 Timothy 3:7) and large groups of people (1 Thessalonians 3:5; Revelation 2:10). He deceives the whole world (Revelation 12:9). Satan accomplishes this by various means, including appealing to the pride of man (1 Timothy 3:6; 1 Corinthians 4:6), interfering with the spread of the truth (Matthew 13:18–22, 38–39), and placing false believers within the church (1 Timothy 4:1–2; 2 Timothy 3:1–9; Revelation 2:9, 3:9). In John 8:44, Jesus says that Satan is a liar and the father of lies. God still grants Satan some authority in this world, which means that his power is not completely destroyed yet, except in one aspect—the power he has of death.

Hebrews 2:14–15 says that Jesus came as a man to die to destroy through death the one who had the empire of death, which is, to the devil, a power that Satan has had from the beginning (John 8:44). The salvation Jesus offers us has freed us from Satan's yoke. Death has already lost its sting (1 Corinthians 15:55).

The power of Satan—the conclusion

The Bible says that the whole world is under the control of the evil one (1 John 5:19), and we must be vigilant and must watch over our adversary. The devil, like a roaring lion, walks around, looking for whom to devour (1 Peter 5:8). Although, Christians have great hope because Jesus Christ (John 16:33) and our faith in him (1 John 5:4) have overcome Satan's wickedness. "Greater is he in us than he who is in the world" (1 John 4:4).

CHAPTER 2

BAD DECISIONS HAVE BAD CONSEQUENCES

At the beginning of creation, the Bible relates that when Adam and Eve were created, they were perfect in every way and literally lived in a paradise known as the garden of Eden (Genesis 2:15). God created man in his image and likeness, which means that they, too, had the freedom to make decisions and choose for their own account. But Genesis 3 describes how Adam and Eve succumbed to the temptations and lies of Satan. When they succumbed, they disobeyed the will of God by eating the fruit of the tree of knowledge, from which they had been forbidden: "And the Lord God commanded the man, 'You are free to eat from any tree in the garden; but you must not eat from the tree of the knowledge of good and evil, for when you eat from it you will certainly die'"(Genesis 2:16–17).

This was the first sin committed by man, which, as a result, subjected the whole human race to both physical and spiritual death by virtue of our inheritance of sin from Adam. As a result of this failure of the first couple, God declared that all who sinned would die, both physically and spiritually. This being the destiny of all mankind.

Let's read the epistle of Saint Paul the apostle to the Romans 5:12: "Therefore, as sin entered the world through one man, and death through sin, so death passed to all men, because all sinned." That first man who had been created in the image and likeness of God, who was a perfect being, lost that likeness by disobeying God. Although by God's mercy, he still retains the image, but the likeness unfortunately disappeared. Since then, our vision of life is twisted and distorted. We cannot deny that, many times, we cling to things that are no more than mere illusions, thinking that they are facts. And we act according to them, to what makes us fall daily in patterns of lives of fantasies and deceptions, so it is necessary that God separate us and free us from conformity and that way of thinking, from those many bad attitudes, and from the negative reactions that surround us.

In truth, it is necessary to free ourselves from all that, immediately straighten our way of thinking and living, organize our minds and hearts, and promptly correct our twisted and tangled relationships. Although, we understand that this is a process that requires patience and infinite love because it is voluntary, which means God never forces us to do anything. But we understand that only those who trust God enough can react positively to his love because they want salvation.

We have to accept that, on many occasions, our knowledge, most of the time, only serves to bring us closer to our ignorance and to which our ignorance brings us even closer to death. But as we approach death, we must be sure whether we will be with God or separated from him.

CHAPTER 3

OUR PROBLEM-FOCUSED SOCIETY

Through our daily lives, when we encounter failures and tragedies that often come our way, there are many people—and we know that this is the case—who begin to wonder if there really is a God who is in control of everything because of the suffering and so many tragedies. For many, this does not make sense. Yes, for many, God is not a God of love or mercy. But in order to truly understand these things and why they happen that way, we must go back to the beginning of Genesis. The Bible tells us of a perfect creation—a creation that was not subject to any kind of pain or suffering or disease and even death (Genesis 1:31).

Now we know very clearly that because of Adam and Eve's disobedience, sin entered with all its consequences (Romans 5:12–21). But the questions still remain: Why, if there really is such a good God, does he allow all these terrible things? Why didn't he reach out with his super powerful hand and deliver us from the consequences of sin? For the benefit of all these people who are navigating in a world of darkness and restlessness, we bring them—this is if they want to accept it, and we hope they do it for the good of their souls—that God did not remove the consequences of sin as such, but it did give us a final exit and a way to escape from any situation no matter how terrible it was (Ephesians 2:12–13). We need to realize that God did it in a way where he first wanted us to see what he was saving us from and in such a way that we would first realize how serious sin is. Through the writings of the Bible, we find the dire consequences of sin. God's absolute will has been that only people without any sin can come before him to enjoy an intimate relationship with him. Ignoring the consequences of sin, such as pain, suffering, and death, even if you don't believe it so, would be a sign of ignorance of mercy and the divine and just nature of God.

The justice and mercy of God are clearly seen in the death and suffering that exist, although many do not want to believe it. The problem is that our society today has focused on the problem itself. Imagine someone who is about to fall down into a deep ravine and is in the midst of that already-tired despair, trying desperately to support himself. We will be surprised to find that if someone tries to reach out to him to save him from an atrocious death, this man, who is at the point of fainting, instead of trying to reach out to the hand of that Samaritan and accept his aid, he will continue to complain about what is happening to him. Instead of accepting that miraculous help, he will start to curse the one who is trying to help him as if this Good Samaritan is the cause of what is happening to him.

It is obvious that by adopting a similar attitude, such a person would be rejecting perhaps the last chance to save his life. Instead of accepting the opportunity that is being presented to you in that moment, where you should be more than grateful and thanking God, you reject that opportunity. The same is true today with the tragedies that surround us. In the Bible, God has offered us a perfect relationship with him, in a perfect state, for all eternity (1 Peter 1:3–5). Compare a lifetime of a relatively few years filled with a little pain and suffering to an eternity enjoying glorious joy in heaven with the Lord (Romans 8:18).

Certainly, we should think twice or more before judging the one who created everything and who is in control of all things. God knows exactly why he allows things to happen. He wants us to see his power and trust him, and above all else, he wants to show us the reality of sin. An example that could help us better understand a part of the purpose that God has in allowing the tragedies that occur daily in our lives is when we stop valuing something that we have every day—electricity, water, or food. They are things that are not appreciated and glorified until we know what it means not to have them. In other words, no one knows what they have until they lose it.

Every time God allows tragedy, we must regard it as merciful calls to repentance. It is God telling us that the consequence of sin is serious. It is God saying that this life is not all there is. It is God saying that he is there and that he wants us to hear him (Romans 2:4–5). Through the Bible, he has revealed to us the way to know him. Faith in the sacrifice of Christ to justify us before God is the best hope that human beings have for the future. We have hope, not just tragedy, pain, and despair.

There is a solution that God has freely offered us. Because we know that to those who love God, all things work together for the good, this is for those who, according to his purpose, are called. What does this mean? This means that neither illness, nor suffering, nor danger, nor pain, nor the spiritual and supernatural, nor problems with others, and nor death itself can separate us from the love of God in Christ Jesus (Romans 8:28–39). God told us that, in this life, there will be suffering and affliction (John 16:33). But he has also promised us that if we trust in the person of his son as our only hope to be justified before God, there is unimaginable glory awaiting us (Titus 3:5–7). In his death, Christ absorbed the consequence of sin so that you and I would not have to suffer it (Galatians 3:13–14). The final and most serious consequence is eternal death without God.

CHAPTER 4

The Voluntary Substitute

In scripture, the death of Christ is revealed as a sacrifice for the sins of the whole world. Accordingly, John the Baptist presented Jesus with the words, "Behold the Lamb of God, who takes away the sin of the world" (John 1:29). Jesus, in his death, was the substitute, dying in the place of all men. Although *substitute* is not specifically a biblical term, the idea that Christ is the substitute for sinners is constantly affirmed in scripture. Through vicarious death, the just and immeasurable judgments of God against the sinner were taken by Christ. The result of this substitution is, in itself, as simple and final as the transaction itself. The Savior has already borne the divine judgments against the sinner to the full satisfaction of God.

To receive the salvation that God offers, mankind is asked to believe this good news, recognizing that Christ died for their sins and thereby claiming Jesus Christ as their personal savior. The word *substitution* only partially expresses everything that took place in the death of Christ. In reality, there is not a term that we could say that captures the whole of that incomparable deed. Popular usage has tried to introduce the word *atonement* for this purpose, but this word does not appear even once in the New Testament. In Hebrews 2:17, this word appears, referring to Christ, but according to its use in the Old Testament, it only means "to cover sin."

> For this reason he had to be made like them, (a)
> fully human in every way, in order that he might

become a merciful and faithful high priest in service to God, and that he might make atonement for the sins of the people. (Hebrews 2:17)

Romans 3:25 says, "God presented Christ as a sacrifice of atonement, through the shedding of his blood—to be received by faith. He did this to demonstrate his righteousness, because in his forbearance he had left the sins committed beforehand unpunished." Although in the times of the Old Testament, nothing more than the sacrifice of an animal was required to remit and conceal sins. God was nonetheless acting in perfect justice in making this requirement since he looked to the manifestation of his lamb, which would come not only to overlook or cover sin but also to remove it once and for all.

Acts 17:30 states, "In the past God overlooked such ignorance, but now he commands all people everywhere to repent." John 1:29 states, "The next day John saw Jesus coming toward him and said, 'Look, the Lamb of God, who takes away the sin of the world!'"

What does the death of the Son entail?

In considering the full value of Christ's death, the following fact should be distinguished: Christ's death assures us of God's love for the sinner.

John 3:16 says, "For God so loved the world that he gave his one and only Son, that whoever believes in him shall not perish but have eternal life."

We read in Romans 5:8, "But God demonstrates his own love for us in this: While we were still sinners, Christ died for us."

1 John 3:16 says, "This is how we know what love is: Jesus Christ laid down his life for us. And we ought to lay down our lives for our brothers and sisters."

1 John 4:9 clearly states, "This is how God showed his love among us: He sent his one and only Son into the world that we might live through him."

And in addition to this, there is, naturally, a reflex action or moral requirement that is projected through this truth regarding divine love onto the lives of the redeemed, but it must not be forgotten that every demand regarding daily conduct is never directed to the unconverted but to those who are already saved in Christ.

We read in 2 Corinthians 5:15, "And he died for all, that those who live should no longer live for themselves but for him who died for them and was raised again."

We see the following in 1 Peter 2:11–25:

> Dear friends, I urge you, as foreigners and exiles, to abstain from sinful desires, which wage war against your soul. Live such good lives among the pagans that, though they accuse you of doing wrong, they may see your good deeds and glorify God on the day he visits us. Submit yourselves for the Lord's sake to every human authority: whether to the emperor, as the supreme authority, or to governors, who are sent by him to punish those who do wrong and to commend those who do right. For it is God's will that by doing good you should silence the ignorant talk of foolish people. Live as free people, but do not use your freedom as a cover-up for evil; live as God's slaves. Show proper respect to everyone, love the family of believers, fear God, honor the emperor. Slaves, in reverent fear of God submit yourselves to your masters, not only to those who are good and considerate, but also to those who are harsh. For it is commendable if someone bears up under the pain of unjust suffering because they are conscious of God. But how is it to your credit if you receive a beating for doing wrong and endure it? But if you suffer for doing good and you endure it, this is commendable before God. To this you

were called, because Christ suffered for you, leaving you an example, that you should follow in his steps. "He committed no sin, and no deceit was found in his mouth." When they hurled their insults at him, he did not retaliate; when he suffered, he made no threats. Instead, he entrusted himself to him who judges justly. "He himself bore our sins" in his body on the cross, so that we might die to sins and live for righteousness; "by his wounds you have been healed." For "you were like sheep going astray," but now you have returned to the Shepherd and Overseer of your souls." The death of Christ is a redemption or ransom payment of God's holy demands for the sinner and to free the sinner from just condemnation. It is significant that the discriminating word "for" means "in place of," or "in favor of," and is used in every passage in the New Testament where the death of Christ is mentioned as a ransom.

Matthew 20:28 says, "Just as the Son of Man did not come to be served, but to serve, and to give his life as a ransom for many."

We read in Mark 10:45, "For even the Son of Man did not come to be served, but to serve, and to give his life as a ransom for many."

In 1 Timothy 2:6, we see, "Who gave himself as a ransom for all people. This has now been witnessed to at the proper time."

CHAPTER 5

BUT WHEN THE FULLNESS
OF TIME WAS COME

The historical aspect of the Bible gives us a lot of information about many events that were recorded at different times, but our main objective is to intertwine the events that pertain to the relationship between God and men through divine revelation so that we finally obtain salvation for the entire human race.

The sacred scriptures indicate that God, at a certain moment, chooses Israel as his people to be the depositary of the divine mission. As a result of this reality, God allows Israel to understand and interpret in a salvific key the historical events they were experiencing. Not because of this decision on the part of God but because of their observed behavior, many times, Israel would have to go from one place to another, time and time again, without a homeland or a fixed home. But God would gather them together anew, and a final restoration would occur. To all this, many precious blessings have been prophesied for the people of Israel as a consequence of the obedience of the people, as there would also be curses that would fall on them for disobeying what was established by God.

However, it is necessary to know that God had previously provided a perfect plan of salvation. For this purpose, God took the form of man in Jesus Christ. Jesus came to this world, as God made flesh, and he dwelled among us as a man. And when he came to where we are, all that he did, as a man, was a perfect sign of obedience to his Father God.

This act on the part of God and his beloved Son, Jesus, was an extraordinary act of salvation for all humanity. Although, unfortunately, there have been, and still even today, people who still believe that salvation is only for a privileged few, especially the Jews who believed that only they were the ones who had the right to God's salvation. There are still passages in the Bible that can be interpreted as that Christ had come only for the Jews. When Christ died and was crucified, he provided salvation for all.

This is what Jesus said: "And I, when I am lifted up from the earth, will draw all people to myself" (John 12:32–33). Throughout their history, the people of Israel have been persecuted, subdued, enslaved, and mistreated. Only for a short period of time did they enjoy the freedom of independence, which they would later lose again. Jehovah, God, in revelation, makes known his will, his purpose in relation to his creation, his actions to rescue a fallen humanity, and everything that mankind needs to know. God reveals and even in advance.

The scriptures reveal that during the time that the Romans ruled over Israel, they made the Jews yearn for the appearance of the Messiah. Let us note that in that important moment in the history of Israel, God took full advantage since it was a good moment for Christ to come. It was so, and we believe it so. According to Galatians chapters 3 and 4, it is well-known that God, according to his will, established a basis through Jewish law to prepare for the coming of the Messiah. God in his sovereignty chose that particular time to send his Son.

We want to point out, before proceeding, that the Bible considers every descendant of Adam to be a fallen sinner, deserving of hell and eternal punishment, and that by grace alone is their only hope. We also want to point out that God the Father is the source of all grace because he designated the eternal covenant of redemption, that God the Son is the only route for the sinner, that the gospel is the promulgator, and that the Holy Spirit is the communicator and applicator of the gospel, cleansing them from the leprosy of sin.

Let's analyze what happened at the particular time that God, in his sovereignty, chose to send his Son to this world. Galatians 4:4 states, "But when the fulness of the time was come, God sent forth his Son, made of a woman, made under the law." This verse makes three important points and tells us that God the Father sent his Son when "the fullness of time came."

Notice the exactness of this writing. In the first part, it indicates to us that was the time of fulfillment when God sent his Son. In the second part, he declares that he was born of a woman, which reminds us of the passage of the conception of Jesus Christ according to the holy gospel according to Saint Luke 1:26–38:

> In the sixth month of Elizabeth's pregnancy, God sent the angel Gabriel to Nazareth, a town in Galilee, to a virgin pledged to be married to a man named Joseph, a descendant of David. The virgin's name was Mary. The angel went to her and said, "Greetings, you who are highly favored! The Lord is with you." Mary was greatly troubled at his words and wondered what kind of greeting this might be. But the angel said to her, "Do not be afraid, Mary; you have found favor with God. You will conceive and give birth to a son, and you are to call him Jesus. He will be great and will be called the Son of the Most High. The Lord God will give him the throne of his father David, and he will reign over Jacob's descendants forever; his kingdom will never end." "How will this be," Mary asked the angel, "since I am a virgin?" The angel answered, "The Holy Spirit will come on you, and the power of the Most High will over-shadow you. So, the holy one to be born will be called the Son of God. Even Elizabeth your relative is going to have a child in her old age, and she who was said to be unable to conceive is in

her sixth month. For no word from God will ever fail." "I am the Lord's servant," Mary answered. "May your word to me be fulfilled." Then the angel left her.

The third point that the verse of Galatians 4:4 declares to us is that Jesus is born under the law. There were many things going on in the age of the first century that, from human reasoning at least, seemed to be ideal for Christ to come. By this time, Rome had unified much of the world under her rule, giving the feeling of unity. At this time, as the empire was relatively at peace, it became possible for the early Christians to travel and thus spread the gospel, which would have been impossible during other times. To all this, while Rome had conquered it militarily, on the other hand, Greece had also done it culturally.

A "common" form of the Greek language (different from classical Greek) was the commercial language, which was spoken throughout the empire, making it easier to communicate the gospel to many different groups of people, through a common language.

The fact that many false idols had "failed" by denying them victory over the Roman conquerors caused many to abandon the worship of those idols. At the same time, in the more "cultured" cities, Greek philosophy and science, of that time, left others spiritually empty in the same way that atheism and communist governments have left a spiritual emptiness in people today. Many of the mysterious religions of that time emphasized a Savior God and required their worshippers to offer them bloody sacrifices, thus making the gospel of Christ, which involved a final sacrifice, credible to them.

The Roman Army recruited soldiers from among the provinces, exposing these men to Roman culture and ideas (such as the gospel) that otherwise would not have reached those distant provinces. The first introduction of the gospel in Great Britain was the result of the effort of Christian soldiers stationed there. These statements are based on man's view of that time and on speculation as to why that particular point in history was a good time for Christ to come and that these may or may not have been some reasons why he chose that particular time to send his Son.

From the context of Galatians chapters 3 and 4, it is evident that God sought to lay a foundation through Jewish law to prepare for the coming of the Messiah. The law was made to help people understand the depth of their sinfulness (in that, they were unable to keep the law) so they could more easily accept the cure for sin through Jesus the Messiah (Galatians 3:22–23; Romans 3:19–20).

The law also served as a "guardian" (Galatians 3:24) to bring people to Jesus as the Messiah. This it did through its many prophecies concerning the Messiah, which were fulfilled in Jesus. Added to this is the sacrificial system, which pointed out the need of a sacrifice for sins as well as its own shortcomings (making each sacrifice always requires the addition of subsequent ones).

Old Testament history also sketched portraits of the person and work of Christ through many religious events and festivals such as Abraham's willingness to sacrifice Isaac or the details of the Passover during the Exodus from Egypt. The time of the incarnation of Christ was such that the people of the time were prepared for his arrival, and from there, the people of each subsequent century have had more than enough evidence that Jesus was really the promised Messiah, having fulfilled the scriptures, which painted and prophesied his arrival in detail.

Therefore, Jesus came and why he died, to become the last and final sacrifice, the perfect sacrifice for our sins (Colossians 1:22; 1 Peter 1:19). Through him, the promise of eternal life with God becomes possible through the faith of those who believe in Jesus so that the promise that is by faith in Jesus Christ would be given to believers (Galatians 3:22). These two words, *faith* and *believe*, are crucial to our salvation. It is through believing in the blood of Christ shed for our sins that we receive eternal life. "For it is by grace you have been saved, through faith—and this is not from yourselves, it is the gift of God—not by works, so that no one can boast" (Ephesians 2:8–9).

CHAPTER 6

THE SEVENTY WEEKS OF DANIEL

Certainly, Christ also came in fulfillment of the specific prophecy. Daniel 9:24–27 speaks of "seventy weeks," or seventy "seven weeks." In this context, these "weeks" or "seven days" refer to groups of seven years (not seven days). When one examines the history and lines up the details of the first sixty-nine weeks, the seventieth week will take place at a future time. The countdown of the seventy weeks begins with "the departure of the order to restore and build Jerusalem" (verse 25). This order was given by Artaxerxes in 445 BC (see Nehemiah 2:5). After seven (sevens) plus sixty-two (sevens) or sixty-nine times seven years, it says that "after the sixty-two 'sevens,' the Anointed One will be put to death and will have nothing. The people of the ruler who will come will destroy the city and the sanctuary. The end will come like a flood: "War will continue until the end, and desolations have been decreed" (which means a greater destruction [verse 26]).

Here we have an unequivocal reference to the death of the Savior crucified on the cross. The writer Sir Robert Anderson in his book *The Coming Prince* gave detailed calculations of the sixty-nine weeks using the prophetic years and considering the leap years, the errors in the calendar, and the change of BC to AD, which is nothing more than before and after Christ. Data concerning this important subject was verified by the scriptures weeks on the same day as Jesus's triumphal entry into Jerusalem and five days before his death. Regardless of whether we use this guide or not, the reality is that the appointed time of Christ's incarnation ties in with this detailed prophecy written by Daniel nearly five hundred years in advance.

We believe that it would be good, even briefly, before finishing this part, to touch on the point of the historical and social context of the life of Jesus. To know a person, it is very important to know the context in which their life has developed. It is not the same to be born in one country than in another, in one culture than in another, or in one political situation that in another. All these circumstances powerfully condition us and shape our mentality.

Jesus was born and lived in a particular situation. He spent most of his life in a small region of eastern Rome called Galilee. At that time, Galilee was a small vassal kingdom of Rome, ruled by one of the sons of Herod the Great named Antipas. It was a relatively prosperous region, but it was under enormous economic and social pressure. Jesus was a Jew, and as such, he had a special relationship with Jerusalem, the holy city, where the temple to which the Jews went on pilgrimage to worship God was located.

Jerusalem is also very important in the life of Jesus because it was there where he died. We are interested in knowing how things were during that time because otherwise we will be continually projecting our way of seeing life on that Jew who lived two thousand years ago in a very distant region and in a culture different from ours. The task is not easy, precisely because of the distance that separates us. We cannot have firsthand information, but we must settle for the archaeological and literary remains that have come down to us in order to reconstruct the "scene" of the life of Jesus. Fortunately, both have been studied with great care and meticulousness, and each time, we have a more accurate picture of the world of Jesus.

CHAPTER 7

UNCERTAIN BIRTH OF JESUS

Although our main focus is the hidden reality surrounding the environment of the crucifixion of Jesus Christ, we do not want to miss the important theme of the birth of Jesus. Because as there is ignorance of his death, so there is regarding his birth. This is the cause of days that are being celebrated, which, in the light of the scriptures, are uncertain. Most people, including most Hebrews, know very little about the Holy Scriptures. Also, too many people know very little about the Christian Bible and therefore do not know any of the information regarding the birth of Jesus Christ.

Yet many (most) genuine Christian believers do not fully understand the Hebrew orientation of Holy Scripture and never make the theological connection between the Judaism of Jesus Christ and its Christian applications. Most customs and traditions, while pious and sincere, are not recognized by God as true worship. In Mark 7:6–7 and Matthew 15:7–9, Christ Jesus said, "Isaiah was right when he prophesied about you hypocrites; as it is written: 'These people honor me with their lips, but their hearts are far from me. They worship me in vain; their teachings are merely human rules.'"

There is always a great danger of not understanding the stories of the Bible when one knows of Christmas carols (folklore based on Roman Catholic myths and fables) better than the Bible itself. One thing is very clear: the time of year that approximately 30 percent of the world's population today celebrates "Christmas," definitively and widely demonstrated, is not the time of year when Christ Jesus was born.

God, the Eternal Father, completed the eternal "Last Word" on this subject almost two thousand years ago. He did not leave his word open for debate. He has only left it open for disbelief or the rejection of lost souls. It is a question of who or what one chooses to believe. Was Jesus born on December 25? The Bible does not reveal exactly what date Jesus was born, and there is no authoritative historical evidence regarding the day or month of Christ's birth. So when was Jesus born? Although the scriptures do not give an explicit answer, many have concluded that it was not December 25 due to very important details, which shed light on the biblical account, and that brings us closer to an understanding in which we will be able to deduce the time in which Jesus was born.

Is Christmas for Christians? Did Jesus's closest disciples celebrate Christmas? What has been discovered is a date prophesied by Haggai five hundred years before Jesus Christ was born. The people in nations with little or no Christian history or tradition celebrate it in increasing numbers. The Gospel of Matthew and the Gospel of Luke are the only two accounts of the birth of Jesus. Both gospels show different perspectives of history. There is no evidence for the exact date of Christ's birth, says the *Holman Concise Bible Dictionary*. Still, around the world, millions of people who call themselves Christians celebrate it on December 25. Since this date does not appear in the Bible, these questions are worth asking:

Why is it so necessary to follow the advice of John chapter 8: "The truth will set you free"? In John 8:31, "Jesus then said to the Jews who had believed in him: If you remain in my word, you will truly be my disciples and you will know the truth, and the truth will set you free." Let's take a look at the honest truth about Christmas. Where did the custom of celebrating Christmas originate? Is it based on the Bible or paganism? In this work, some truths about Christmas are revealed. But before going any further, let's analyze the prophecy of Haggai chapter 2:

> Who is left among you that saw this house in her
> first glory? and how do ye see it now? is it not in

your eyes in comparison of it as nothing? Yet now be strong, O Zerubbabel, saith the Lord; and be strong, O Joshua, son of Josedech, the high priest; and be strong, all ye people of the land, saith the Lord, and work: for I am with you, saith the Lord of hosts: According to the word that I covenanted with you when ye came out of Egypt, so my spirit remaineth among you: fear ye not. For thus saith the Lord of hosts; Yet once, it is a little while, and I will shake the heavens, and the earth, and the sea, and the dry land; And I will shake all nations, and the desire of all nations shall come: and I will fill this house with glory, saith the Lord of hosts. The silver is mine, and the gold is mine, saith the Lord of hosts. The glory of this latter house shall be greater than of the former, saith the Lord of hosts: and in this place will I give peace, saith the Lord of hosts. In the four and twentieth day of the ninth month, in the second year of Darius, came the word of the Lord by Haggai the prophet, saying, etc.

We hope that you will analyze well chapter 2 of the prophet Haggai. In this chapter, you will find especially these verses, which we will give you a short review guided by the Holy Spirit so that we can understand them better. Chapter 2 of Haggai consists of five hundred years before the birth of the baby Jesus. And they are considered double-reference verses. Let us first analyze the second universal epistle of Saint Peter the apostle chapter 3, verse 8: "But do not forget this one thing, dear friends: With the Lord a day is like a thousand years, and a thousand years are like a day." Considering what Peter says, if Haggai spoke five hundred years ago, the birth in this double reference was announced. Let's read Haggai 2:6. "This is what the Lord Almighty says: 'In a little while I will once more shake the heavens and the earth, the sea and the dry land. I will shake all

nations, and what is desired by all nations will come, and I will fill
this house with glory,' says the Lord Almighty." It is clear that this
quote refers to the first coming of Christ to earth. Let us now analyze
the first part of verse 10: "On the twenty-fourth day of the ninth
month, in the second year of Darius, the word of the Lord came to
the prophet Haggai."

"On the 24th day of the ninth month." Here, this quotation
is interpreted with double reference, and very clearly, it says the
twenty-fourth day of the ninth month—a date that can vary in
some years. Many, I have even heard take an account to reach the
ninth month, and it begins from the month of January, ending in
the month of September. It is a mistake to do so because the correct
way is according to the Jewish calendar, which begins in the month
of April. But counting from April, we also find another problem,
and that is that many count as, "April, one. May, two. June, three.
July, four. August, five. September, six. October, seven. November,
eight. December, nine." But this is not the correct way to count
either. That is why the majority, when counting like this, end in
December and assure that Jesus was born on December 24. But
please pay close attention. We must remember that in the Jewish
Calendar, the months of July and August do not exist because the
month of July was added to our calendar in honor of Julius Caesar
and the month of August was also added to our calendar in honor of
Augustus Caesar. In other words, the correct way is as follows: From
April to May, one month. From May to June, two months. From
June to September, three months. From September to October,
four months. From October to November, five months. From
November to December, six months. From December to January,
seven months. From January to February, eight months. And from
February to March, nine months. It means that the exact count is,
on the twenty-fourth day of the ninth month. It has been March
24. This is the approximate date that the Child Jesus was born. Let
us also remember that some dates vary during the years. In other
words, an event may fall in a certain month, and in another year, it
may fall in another month.

Let's start with something from the manger. Because we are already living in the end-times, God is bringing to light and revealing many mysteries and establishing his truths so that no one has an excuse for their salvation. Let's meditate on this in relation to the birth of Jesus. What animals were present in the manger? Our position is that, at the time Jesus was born, there were no animals in the manger. In part of our investigations, we found that the manger was a hut placed behind the inn where food was kept for the animals of the strangers who came to stay. It could be that there was room for shelter for animals at night, as tradition relates, but at that time of the birth of Jesus, there were no animals in that place. In this case, the gospel does not speak of animals. Reading the Old and New Testaments, related to each other, it has filled this gap very soon, referring to Isaiah 1:3 "The ox knows its master, the donkey its owner's manger."

Not quite. The biblical account never makes mention of a stable or a cave. This is usually assumed due to the manger mentioned. But in the ancient world, as in many primitive modern cultures, mangers were a common part of the home. The animals are even kept inside the same house at night, for when the animals were brought inside. Also, some houses in the mountainous region of Judea were built alongside the hillside, so the lower level could have been a cave with a house built over it.

Let's learn a little about the origin of the current manger that we know of according to the story of the manger. Do you know who brought up the idea of the manger? This idea was introduced by Saint Francis of Assisi known as the saint of humility and poverty, at Christmas 1223, many years ago, in the small town of Greccio in Italy. By this time, there was a great devotion to the cradle but at no time was it correct that there were animals at the time of the birth of Jesus. It was Saint Francis of Assisi who popularized the idea of the manger and gave it the tangible form in which it is known today. When Saint Francis visited Rome in 1223, he informed Pope Honorius III of his plans to make a stage performance of the nativity site. The pope gladly listened to the details of the project and approved it. Having left Rome, Saint Francis arrived in Greccio on Christmas Eve, and it was then that, with the help of his friend Giovanni Velita, he built a cradle and grouped around it the images of Mary, Joseph, the donkey, the ox, and the shepherds who worshipped the newborn Savior. On one occasion, Pope Benedict XVI, in his book, postulated that these animals were not present at the birth of Bethlehem. However, he maintained that Jesus was born in Bethlehem at a certain time, and his mother was a virgin chosen by God, just as the Bible says. The pope also said that the role of the donkey and the ox, always strategically located to give warmth to the child God, had to change completely, since he affirmed, as we have already indicated, that these animals were not present in the manger. The pope also questioned the date of Jesus's birth and other arguments.

Do you know the origin of the Christmas tree of Santa Claus and of the Christmas bonus exchange? It was Christmas Eve. The children had made the manger and were eagerly awaiting the arrival of Santa Claus loaded with gifts. At dawn on December 25, they found a large number of packages with toys and sweets under a brand-new Christmas tree. Their parents assured them that all this had been brought by Santa Claus during the night while they slept. Did children doubt what their parents told them? Of course not! They took it for granted. Didn't the same thing happen to you? Very few have stopped to think why they believe what they believe and why they observe certain customs. Most of us learned to accept everything without hesitation. Why is this happening? By sheepish instinct? Not quite. By nature, we have a tendency to do what others do even if they are wrong. The sheep follow the flock to the slaughterhouse. But humans must watch where we are going.

CHAPTER 8

WHAT WAS THE ORIGIN
OF CHRISTMAS?

Is Christmas really the celebration of the birth of Jesus Christ? Was Jesus born on December 25? The original apostles, who knew Jesus personally and were instructed by him, did they celebrate his birthday on December 25? Did the idea ever occur to you? If Christmas is the most important holiday in Christianity, why do so many non-Christians observe it? Do you know?

Why is it a time to exchange gifts with our relatives and friends? Does this custom originate from the magi who presented gifts to the baby Jesus? The answers may surprise us. Most people assume many things about Christmas—things that are not really true. But let's not assume anything but rather look for the facts.

This festival made its appearance in the Catholic Church, and from there, it spread to Protestantism and the rest of the world. Now where did the Catholic Church get it from? It was not from the teachings of the New Testament; it was not from the Bible or the apostles who had been personally instructed by Jesus Christ. Christmas was introduced into the church during the fourth century from paganism.

Since the celebration of Christmas was introduced into the world by the Roman Catholic Church and has no other authority than its own, let us see what the *Catholic Encyclopedia* (1911 edition) says about it: "Christmas was not included among the first festivals of the church. The first signs of it come from Egypt. Pagan customs related to the beginning of January centered on the feast of Christmas."

In the same encyclopedia, under "Natal Day," we find that Origen, one of the fathers of the church, recognized the following truth: "We do not see in the scriptures that anyone has kept a feast or celebrated a great banquet on the day of his birth. Only sinners (like Pharaoh and Herod) celebrated with great rejoicing the day they were born into this world."

The *Encyclopedia Britannica*, 1946 edition, says, "Christmas was not counted among the ancient festivities of the church." It was not instituted by Jesus Christ or by the apostles or by biblical authority. It was later borrowed from paganism. The *Encyclopedia Americana*, 1944 edition, says, "Christmas, according to many authorities, was not celebrated in the first centuries of the Christian Church, since the custom of Christianity, in general, was to celebrate not the birth but the death of important people. (The Communion, or rather, Easter, instituted by biblical authority in the New Testament, is a commemoration of the death of Christ.)

In memory of this event (the birth of Christ), a festival was instituted in the fourth century. In the fifth century, the Western Church ordered that it be celebrated forever on the same day as the ancient Roman holiday in honor of the birth of the sun, since the exact date of the birth of Christ was not known. Let us take note of this important fact. These historical authorities show that during the first two or three centuries of our era, Christians did not celebrate Christmas. This holiday was introduced into the Roman Church in the fourth century AD, and it was not until the fifth century that it was established as an official Christian holiday!

Jesus was not born on December 25. Jesus Christ was not even born at the time of year when Christmas is now observed! When he was born, there were shepherds in the same region who watched and kept the night watches over their flock (Luke 2:8). This could never have happened in Judea in the month of December. Shepherds brought their flocks from the fields and locked them up no later than mid-October to protect them from the approaching cold and rainy season. The Bible itself proves, in Song of Songs 2:11 and Ezra 10:9–13, that winter was the rainy season, which made it impossible for the shepherds to stay in the field at night with their flocks.

"It was an ancient custom of the Jews of those times to take their flocks out into the fields and deserts around Passover (early spring) and bring them home again at the beginning of the first rains" (*Adam Clarke's Commentary on the Bible*, volume 5, page 370). The same commentator states, "The shepherds watched their flocks, day and night, while they were outside. Since the first rain fell at the beginning of the month of Chesvan, which corresponds to part of the months of October and November (it starts in October), we see that the herds stayed in the field all summer." Now, according to the biblical account, the shepherds had not yet gathered their flocks, which leads us to suppose that the month of October had not yet begun and that, therefore, our Lord was not born on December 25, when there were no flocks in fields. He could not have been born after September since the herds were still in the field at night. With this, we must rule out the nativity in December. The night grazing of the herds in the fields is a chronological fact.

Any encyclopedia or other authority can confirm the fact that Christ was not born on December 25. The *Catholic Encyclopedia* says it clearly that the exact date of the birth of Jesus Christ is totally unknown. This is recognized by all authorities. The lack of space in this publication prevents us from displaying the scriptures indicating that this event happened in early fall, possibly in the month of September, about six months after Easter.

If God had wanted us to keep and celebrate the birthday of Jesus Christ, he would not have hidden the date. How did he get into the church? How could this pagan festival get into the western Christian world? The *New Schaff-Herzog Encyclopedia of Religious Knowledge* makes this clear in its article on Christmas: "It cannot be precisely determined to what extent the date of this holiday depended on the pagan Brumaría (December 25), which followed Saturnalia (December 17–24) and commemorated the shortest day of the year and the new sun." The pagan festivals of Saturnalia and

Brumaría were too deeply rooted in popular customs to be suppressed by Christian influence. The pagan festival, with its uproar and merriment, was so popular that Christians were pleased to see an excuse to continue celebrating it without major changes in the spirit and manner of its observance.

Christian preachers from the West and the Near East protested against the unseemly frivolity with which the birth of Christ was celebrated, while the Christians of Mesopotamia accused their Western brethren of idolatry and sun worship for accepting this pagan holiday as Christian.

Remember that the Roman world had been pagan. Before the fourth century, Christians were few, though their numbers were increasing and they were persecuted by the government and the pagans. But with the advent of Emperor Constantine, who in the fourth century declared himself a Christian and raised Christianity to a level of equality with paganism, the Roman world began to accept this popularized Christianity and new adherents numbered in the hundreds of thousands.

Let us bear in mind that these people had been educated in pagan customs, the main one being that idolatrous festival of December 25. It was a joyous party and had a special spirit. The people liked it! They didn't want to suppress it! The article already quoted from the *New Schaff-Herzog Encyclopedia of Religious Knowledge* explains how Constantine's recognition of Sunday, a day when pagans previously worshipped the sun, and how the influence of pagan Manichaeism, which identified the son of God with the sun, gave reason to these pagans of the fourth century, now converted en masse to Christianity, to accommodate their pagan festival of December 25 (the day of the birth of the Sun God) the title of the day of the birth of the son of God.

This is how Christmas was introduced in our western world. Although we give it another name, it is still the same pagan festival of worship to the sun. Only the name has changed. We can call a hare "lion," but it is not for this reason that it ceases to be a hare. The *Encyclopedia Britannica* says, "From the year 354, some Latins may have moved the date from January 6 to December 25, which was then a Mithraic feast or birthday of the invincible sun. On January 6, they accused the Romans of idolaters and worshippers of the sun, maintaining that the festival of December 25 had been invented by the disciples of Corinthians.

CHAPTER 9

IS THE DATE OF JESUS'S
BIRTH WRONG?

As we have already explained, the true origin of Christmas comes from ancient Babylon. It is engulfed in the organized apostasy that has kept the world deceived for many centuries! In Egypt, it was always believed that the son of Isis (Egyptian name for the "queen of heaven") was born on December 25. Pagans throughout the known world celebrated this date centuries before the birth of Jesus Christ. Jesus, the true Messiah, was not born on December 25. The apostles and the early church never celebrated the birthday of Christ on that date or any other. There is no mandate or instruction in the Bible to do so. But there is a command to observe, not celebrate, the date of his death (1 Corinthians 11:24–26; John 13:14–17).

Thus, it was that the Chaldean Mysteries, invented by Nimrod's wife, were bequeathed to us with new Christian names by pagan religions. Other pagan customs, in addition to the traditional Christmas customs of our towns, we have adopted others that, despite being of pagan origin, achieve an enthusiastic reception. The "Christmas flower" and the wood that is lit in the fireplace are "vestiges of pre-Christian times," according to the *Encyclopedia Americana*. The green crown or garland that adorns the doors of so many homes are equally pagan. Frederic J. Haskins addresses it in his book *Answers to Questions*: "It goes back to the pagan customs of decorating buildings and places of worship for the holiday that was celebrated at the same time as Christmas. The Christmas tree comes from Egypt and its origin predates the Christian era."

Even the candles, a traditional symbol of Christmas, are an old pagan custom, as they were lit at sunset to revive the Sun God when he was extinguished to make way for night. Also, the Father Christmas or Santa Claus is the same Saint Nicholas, Catholic bishop of the fifth century.

The *Encyclopedia Britannica*, 11th edition, volume 19, pages 648–649, says,

> Saint Nicholas, Bishop of Mira, saint venerated by the Greeks and Latins on December 6. It is said that a legend according to which he clandestinely gave gifts to the three daughters of a poor citizen gave rise to the custom of secretly giving gifts on the eve of Saint Nicholas day (December 6), a date that was later changed to the day of Christmas. Hence the association of Christmas with Santa Claus.

Parents punish their children for telling lies, but when Christmas comes, they themselves are responsible for telling them the lie of Santa Claus, the three wise men, or the Child God. So why is it surprising that when they reach adulthood, they also believe that God is a myth? A certain boy, feeling sadly disappointed when he learned the truth, commented to a little friend, "Yes, and I am also going to find out about this Jesus Christ!" Is it Christian to teach children myths and lies? God says, "You shall not deceive or lie to each other" (Leviticus 19:11).

Although it may seem good to the human mind and it will try to justify it, God also says, "There is a way that seems right to man, but its end is the way of death." Studying the facts, then we see with amazement that the custom of celebrating Christmas is actually not Christian but pagan. It makes it one of the ways of Babylon that the world has fallen into! Is the exchange of gifts biblical? For some people, this is the most important point of everything when it comes to the observance of Christmas—the time to buy and exchange gifts. In this regard, many will exclaim triumphantly, "For this, we do have biblical authorization! Didn't Jesus Christ at birth receive gifts from the magi?"

Again, the truth has a surprise for us. First, let's look at the historical origin of the custom of giving Christmas gifts and then see what the Bible tells us about it. We quote the following from the *Sacred Library*, volume 12, pages 153–155: "The exchange of gifts between friends is characteristic of both Christmas and Saturnalia and the Christians surely took it from the pagans, as the admonition clearly shows of Tertullian."

The truth is that the custom of exchanging gifts with friends and relatives during the Christmas season has absolutely nothing to do with Christianity! Strange as it may seem to us, they do not celebrate the birth of Jesus Christ or honor him! Suppose someone you love is celebrating his birthday. Would you honor her by buying lots of gifts for all your other relatives and friends, ignoring the person you want to honor? Doesn't it seem absurd from this point of view?

Yet this is precisely what people all over the world do. They observe a day when Christ was not born, spending all the money they can raise to give gifts to their relatives and friends. But years of experience teach us that professing Christians often forget to give something to Christ and his work in the month of December. This is usually the month when God's work suffers the most. Apparently, people are so busy exchanging Christmas gifts that they don't remember Christ or his work. Then during January and even February, they try to get back everything they spent on Christmas so that many, in terms of their support for Christ and his work, do not return to normal until March.

Let's see what the Bible says in Matthew 2:1–11 regarding the gifts that the magi brought when Jesus Christ was born: "When Jesus was born in Bethlehem of Judea in the days of King Herod, some magi came from the east to Jerusalem, saying, Where is the king of the Jews, who was born?" As a clarifying note, when you read

Matthew chapter 2 onwards, there you will find that those magi, who were not three, was a caravan that came from the east and that they were not kings, to which we wonder where the names of Gaspar, Melchor, and Baltazar came from because the Bible does not mention a name and neither does it say that they were kings so that they are called the three holy kings. This is a mere lie that, for many years, has been practiced and has deceived poor children.

Another thing we want to point out is that in verse 11 of the same chapter of Matthew, the wise men, after asking King Herod where the child was and after Herod explained it to them, followed the star, finding the child in a house and not in the manger. By that time, the child was more or less one and a half to two years old because then you can see that Herod felt that he was being mocked by the wise men, because they had a vision where they were alerted not to return to Herod because he wanted to kill the child. Herod furiously ordered to kill all the children two years and under. Well, as we have already mentioned, when the wise men entered the house, they saw the child with his mother Mary. And falling down, they adored him; and opening their treasures, they offered him presents: gold, frankincense, and myrrh. Why did they bring Christ gifts? Note that the wise men asked about the baby Jesus, born king of the Jews. But why did they bring him gifts? Because it's his birthday? No way! They arrived more like a year after his birth.

So did they do it to set an example for us? No! Let's take note. They did not exchange gifts, rather they "offered presents" to him, to Christ. They did not exchange gifts with their friends and family or with one another! Why? The aforementioned *Adam Clarke's Commentary on the Bible*, volume 5, page 46, verse 11 says, "They offered him presents." In the East, it is not customary to enter the presence of kings and great personages empty-handed. This custom is mentioned frequently in the Old Testament and still persists in the East and in some islands of the Pacific.

CHAPTER 10

NIMROD'S APPEARANCE

The chapters of the Bible that relate genealogies seem very boring, monotonous, and of little importance to many people. Perhaps you find it difficult to stay focused when reading a list of names that seems to have no end. The sons of Fulano were Mengano, Zutano, and Perencejo; the sons of Mengano were Perengano and Citano. The sons of Perencejo were these, those, and others; but the sacred writers included such information for a special purpose.

Genesis 10 is one of these chapters that follow this same genealogical format. Its verses narrate the origin of the nations after the flood and is the account of the new beginning of humanity that begins with the three sons of Noah: Shem, Ham, and Japheth. However, when we get from verse 8 to 12, we find a little parenthesis about a character named Nimrod. Why is it that the author dedicates five verses to this character? Who is this guy?

Nimrod was the great-grandson of Noah and the grandson of Ham. At first glance, he seems to have several positive qualities. He was powerful and vigorous and was a hunter and the founder of several cities. His name, which means "tyrant" or "rebel" is mentioned only four times in the entire Bible—twice in the aforementioned passage, once in first Chronicles as part of the genealogy, and one last time in Micah when it refers to the land of Nimrod.

Nimrod was actually the first dictator on earth, and according to rabbinic literature, he caused people to rebel against God. He was also the founder of two great cities, Babel and Nineveh, which became great empires that, many years later, conquered the divided kingdom of Israel. Nimrod introduced a religious system based on astrology and the occult. We can see this in the construction of the Tower of Babel, which was a temple or ziggurat where the sun and the moon were worshipped. Nimrod and his wife, Semiramis, lived after the Great Flood. The name *Semiramis* does not appear in the Bible. Nimrod was Noah's great-grandson. Nimrod's lineage is as follows: Noah begot Ham, Ham to Cush, and Cush to Nimrod. "He was a mighty hunter before Jehovah." This, that is related to him makes us think of the Syrian king Tiglath-Pileser I since he also had a reputation as a great hunter, killing 120 lions in hand-to-hand combat and 800 from his cart.

This male Nimrod "became the first mighty one on earth." His name is a translation of the Hebrew *Gibor*, which means "tyrant" or "rebel." These data points indicate that he was a strong man of character, rebellious before the true Creator God. "He was a mighty hunter before Jehovah," but "before Jehovah" does not mean "according to the will or purpose of Jehovah," Keil and Delitzsch point out in their great work. His name *Marad* in Hebrew means "we will rebel," indicating "violent resistance against God."

Nimrod established several cities, including Babel in the land of Shinar, and Nineveh, which, centuries later, was the capital of the Assyrian Kingdom. The name *Nineveh* is derived from "Nina," the name of a goddess who was later called Ishtar. Originally established by Nimrod and known today as Nimrud, Calah became a major city in Iraq.

In her first appearance in the world, the great harlot sits on Sumer-Chaldea. It does so through the person of Semiramis, Nimrod's wife, that is, the great harlot personifies herself in Semiramis. Diodorus, a Greek man of Cecilia, tells the story of Semiramis. When Nimrod died, Semiramis proclaimed herself "Rhea," that is, "mother of the gods."

Let's take note: "Mother of the gods" is a very notable and common distinctive in the annals of the human race. Later in the story, Nimrod, now dead but not forgotten, became known as Baal, a title that means "lord" or "master." They also called him Kronos. The Romans called him Saturn. Semiramis, being the wife of Baal, her title would have been Baalti. Translated into Latin, Baalti means "dominates me." With this translated into Italian, the name or title is "Madonna." Following the idolatrous tradition originated in Sumeria-Chaldea, the Roman Catholic Church calls Mary "the Madonna," a title that is never conferred on her in the Bible.

Thus, the linguistic links forge an indisputable link between the very ancient mother goddess Baalti (Semiramis) and the Madonna of Roman Catholicism. What researcher, historian, or theologian can prove that this is not how we present it? We confidently affirm that multitudes of Roman Catholics, by venerating the Virgin Mary (the Madonna) with a fervor that surpasses their worship of Christ, continue to spread among human beings, without the vast majority realizing what they do, the ancient idolatrous concept of a powerful "pagan mother goddess," "mother of the gods."

The perceptive student of human history and the book of Revelation do not overlook such an obviously strong connection between the paganism of ancient Sumer-Chaldea and the Mariology of the Roman Catholic Church. Returning to Semiramis, she claimed that her son Tammuz had been miraculously born, claiming that he was the reincarnation of Nimrod. The classical writers identify Tammuz as Bacus, a name that means "lamented son."

This lamented son is associated by some with the prophecy of Genesis 3:15. The resemblance between Tammuz and Christ is evident. Of both, it is said that his birth was miraculous. "Lamented son" or "son of suffering" is applied to both. One of the two is a false messiah. Born to a woman who had the audacity to call herself mother of the gods, Tammuz is the fake. Christ, and not Tammuz (Bacus), is the one who fulfills Genesis 3:15. It is theorized that Semiramis played an important role in the development of the Chaldean Mysteries, those that served to spread the idolatry that she fomented. Semiramis, in the mythological character of the goddess Isis (Helen), appears in a Samaritan sect organized by Simon the Magician.

Clearly, Osiris was Nimrod, and Isis was Semiramis. Thus, Simon the Magician said that he himself had been the power that moved Nimrod and that Helen was Semiramis, the queen of heaven.

CHAPTER 11

NIMROD'S ABERRANT SIN

Christmas is one of the mainstays of the corrupt system called Babylon, and as such, it is censured in the prophecies and biblical teachings. It has its roots in the ancient Babylon of Nimrod! Yes, it dates from the time immediately after the flood! Nemrod or Nimrod was a mystical monarch of Mesopotamia, mentioned in chapter 10 of the book of Genesis, who also appears in numerous legends and stories. Nimrod, grandson of Ham, son of Noah, was the true founder of the Babylonian system—a system of organized competition, of empires and human governments, and of the economic system of profit—which has taken over the world ever since.

Nimrod built the Tower of Babel, the original Babylon, Nineveh, and many other cities. He organized the first kingdom of this world. The name *Nimrod* is derived from the Hebrew word *marad*, which means "to rebel." From ancient writings, we learn that it was this man who began the great organized world apostasy that has dominated the world from time immemorial until now. Nimrod was so wicked that he is said to have married his own mother whose name was Semiramis. According to belief, she became pregnant.

According to historians, when Nimrod died, his wife, Queen Semiramis, proclaimed him the Sun God, also known as the god Baal. Semiramis then had an illegitimate son named Tammuz, and she declared that this child was miraculously conceived through the spirit of her deceased husband in an immaculate conception.

Semiramis also stated that her son was actually the return or rebirth of her husband, Nimrod, and this is how the doctrine of reincarnation originated.

Before long, the followers of Nimrod also began to worship the mother more than the son, venerating her as the queen of heaven and the goddess of fertility. Semiramis was known by other names such as Astarte, Inanna, and Ishtar (or "Easter" in English). If this cult of mother and child sounds familiar, it is because Catholicism is based on these pagan traditions, and the person responsible for this idolatry is Nimrod.

After his premature death, his so-called mother-wife, Semiramis, propagated the perverse doctrine of Nimrod's survival as a spiritual being. She claimed that overnight a large tree (evergreen type) grew out of a dead stump, symbolizing Nimrod's birth to a new life. She stated that on each birthday anniversary, Nimrod would leave gifts in the tree. The date of his birth was December 25. Here is the true origin of the Christmas tree. With plots and intrigues, Semiramis became the Babylonian queen of heaven, and Nimrod, under various names, became the divine son of heaven.

After several generations of this idolatrous worship, Nimrod also became the false messiah, son of Baal, and the Sun God. In this false Babylonian system, the mother and the son (Semiramis and Nimrod born again) became the main objects of worship. This veneration of mother and child spread throughout the world with variations of names according to countries and languages. As surprising as it may seem, we find ourselves the equivalent of the Madonna long before the birth of Jesus Christ!

Thus it was that in the fourth and fifth centuries, while the pagans of the Roman world were converting en masse to Christianity, taking with them their ancient pagan beliefs and customs and disguising them under Christian names. The idea of mother and child also became popular, especially around Christmastime. Christmas cards, Christmas carols, and manger scenes reflect this same theme.

Those of us who were raised in this Babylonian world, who have listened to and accepted these things throughout our lives, have learned to worship them as sacred. We never doubt. We never stopped to investigate whether these customs had their origin in the Bible or in pagan idolatry.

CHAPTER 12

THE TRUE ORIGIN OF CHRISTMAS

So we have seen that Christmas came into the world through the Catholic Church and that they received it from paganism. However, where did the pagans get it? What was its true origin? At this time, it is normal to talk about these issues. Who have ever asked themselves, how did the Christmas tree come about? One of the most characteristic elements of Christmas is undoubtedly the tree. Decorated with ribbons, colored balls, lights, and other ornamentation, the tree contributes to giving a Christmas image wherever it is placed. Many are the places where the starting gun for Christmas is set off by turning on the lights of the tree. Although there are several theories about the origin of the Christmas tree, one of the most widespread postulates is that it comes from the Celts of Central Europe, who used trees to represent various gods. In addition, coinciding with the date of Christian Christmas, they celebrated the birth of Frey, god of the sun and fertility, by decorating a tree. It had the name Divine Yggdrasil (tree of the universe). In its crown was heaven, and in the deep roots was hell. According to legend, between the years 680 and 754, Saint Boniface, evangelizer of Germany, understood that it was impossible to uproot this pagan tradition, so he decided to adapt it by giving it a Christian meaning. This is how he cut down an oak tree with an ax.

It represented Odin, and in its place, he planted a pine tree, which, being perennial, symbolized the love of God, adorning it with apples and candles. The apples represented original sin, and the candles, the light of Jesus Christ.

Later, with the evangelization to these people, Christians took up the idea of the tree to celebrate the birth of Christ. It is believed that the first Christmas tree, as we know it today, appeared in Germany in 1605. The custom of decorating trees to welcome the Christmas season took root in Germany and Scandinavia in the seventeenth century, and it was carried by the sovereigns of the Hannover house to Great Britain in the eighth century. George III, crowned sovereign of England in 1762, and his wife, Queen Charlotte, a native of Germany, were the first to adorn their palace with a domestic fir. Although it was not until half a century later that good English society fell, enchanted by the idea of reproducing in their homes what their eyes had seen in Windsor Palace. It was inhabited then by the sovereign Victoria and her husband, Prince Albert of Saxe-Coburg—a German nobleman who introduced the tree as the latest Christmas fad in Victorian society shortly after marrying the queen in 1840.

Albert of Saxony (born in Coburg) brought with him to England the memory of a country in which, around the seventeenth century, families began to gather around a Christmas tree. How can we forget those days when some German families, after looking for an excuse for the children to leave the house, took advantage of their absence to decorate the tree with fruits and toys on that same day, December 24? How can we also forget the ancient Germanic belief that it was a gigantic tree that supported the world and supported (this explains the custom of putting lights on trees), in its branches, the weight of the moon, the sun, and the stars? A tree that was also the symbol of life since, in winter, when almost all nature appeared dead, it did not lose its green foliage. The origin of the Christmas tree is older than the birth of Jesus Christ. It entered between the second and third millennium BC.

At that time, a great variety of Indo-European people who were expanding throughout Europe and Asia considered trees as an expression of energy and fertility that Mother Nature had. For this reason, they worshipped them. One of the trees that were considered the most beautiful was the oak, which was considered the king of trees.

In winter, when the leaves fell, the ancient people used to put various ornaments in the tree. All of this was to attract the spirits of nature, who were thought to have fled there. The modern Christmas tree appeared in Germany; it was made popular in the sixteenth century. It was from the nineteenth century that the tradition reached England, France, the United States, and Puerto Rico. And later, in the twentieth century, it became a tradition in Spain and Latin America.

Now that you know why the Christmas trees exist, it now only depends on you if you want to continue worshipping the spirits of nature. Let's now get ready, and please take a very careful look at what we will find next in these upcoming important chapters. Although, we consider that all are important. Possibly, you are in one way or another familiar with what we will be presenting, and if not, enjoy it.

CHAPTER 13

WHO CARRIED THE CROSS THAT WAS USED TO CRUCIFY CHRIST, JESUS, OR SIMON OF CYRENE?

With this work that we are presenting here, we are not trying to establish a precedent; in other words, we are not trying to make a milestone in history because we are aware that, although not many, there are people who have more or less the same interpretation that we have. Now yes, obeying the mandate that God has given us to preach this gospel in and out of time, we want to deeply analyze and answer with biblical support this following question:

Who carried the cross, Jesus or Simon of Cyrene? We can say, without fear of being wrong, that in many parts of the world, the event better known as Holy Week is celebrated and is also known by many as La Semana Mayor. To carry out this celebration, there are processions of crowds that carry a statue in the resemblance of Christ with an appearance on his face of deep suffering and carrying a heavy wooden cross on his shoulders.

Now as a result of a meticulous investigation of the biblical writings in relation to this momentous event, we find and firmly establish, without any doubt, that Christ, in the spiritual part as God, could have endured everything that entailed confronting the crucifixion without any problem. But it was necessary and thus established by God himself in complete agreement with his own son Jesus Christ that, although he was the son of God, it was necessary for him to take a human body and thus face this inhuman challenge that he had to go through for all of us.

Let us not forget that Christ went through all this sacrifice in his human nature, and after having gone through terrible moments of suffering, having his back destroyed, having his entire face disfigured, and having so many abuses to his body, he was not, in the least, to suffer from physical exhaustion, where naturally all his strength was exhausted. Analyzing all this picture of suffering that Christ had to go through, do not believe that there were too many overwhelming tests to be able to reach the conclusive statement that he could have carried the timber in that disastrous condition in which he, as human, was in. As God, yes, but as a human, the situation was very difficult. This unequaled sacrifice made by Christ in favor of humanity, a sacrifice that the Lord Jesus made for sinful humanity, began from the moment he left the same right hand of the Father, as it is shown in many passages, a sacrifice none too great for the Lord to show his love for all humanity.

And we know from his word that everything was fulfilled according to the plan of salvation, even giving his life on the cross of Calvary, according to what is found in the book of the prophet Isaiah. And it would be better to take a look at some of these passages:

Sufferings of the servant of the Lord

> See, my servant will act wisely he will be raised and lifted up and highly exalted. Just as there were many who were appalled at him[c]—his appearance was so disfigured beyond that of any human being and his form marred beyond human likeness—so he will sprinkle many nations, and kings will shut their mouths because of him. For what they were not told, they will see, and what they have not heard, they will understand. (Isaiah 52:13–15)

Who has believed our message and to whom has the arm of the Lord been revealed? He grew up before him like a tender shoot, and like a root out of dry ground. He had no beauty or majesty to attract us to him, nothing in his appearance that we should desire him. He was despised and rejected by mankind, a man of suffering, and familiar with pain. Like one from whom people hide their faces he was despised, and we held him in low esteem. Surely he took up our pain and bore our suffering, yet we considered him punished by God, stricken by him, and afflicted. But he was pierced for our transgressions, he was crushed for our iniquities; the punishment that brought us peace was on him, and by his wounds we are healed. We all, like sheep, have gone astray, each of us has turned to our own way; and the Lord has laid on him the iniquity of us all. He was oppressed and afflicted, yet he did not open his mouth; he was led like a lamb to the slaughter, and as a sheep before its shearers is silent, so he did not open his mouth. By oppression and judgment he was taken away. Yet who of his generation protested? For he was cut off from the land of the living; for the transgression of my people he was punished. He was assigned a grave with the wicked, and with the rich in his death, though he had done no violence, nor was any deceit in his mouth. Yet it was the Lord's will to crush him and cause him to suffer, and though the Lord makes his life an offering for sin, he will see his offspring and prolong his days, and the will of the Lord will prosper in his hand. After he has suffered, he will see the light of life and be satisfied; by his knowledge my righteous servant

will justify many, and he will bear their iniquities. Therefore I will give him a portion among
the great, and he will divide the spoils with the
strong, because he poured out his life unto death,
and was numbered with the transgressors. For he
bore the sin of many and made intercession for
the transgressors. (Isaiah 53:1–12)

With all the above presented here and regarding that, if Christ
truly carried the cross, they imagine Christ carrying a heavy cross,
exhausted and injured by the falls under the heavy wood that hurt his
shoulders with every step he took while he was hit by the Romans.
On the other hand, we want to introduce you to another phrase of
the followers of the Roman Catholic Church. That is, his hands held
the cross, and he fell with it three times. As it is also very repetitive to
hear from some preachers say, "When Christ was taken to be crucified, he felt the terrible weight of that terrible cross when he carried
it on his shoulders."

We ask, Do you really believe that Christ carried the cross? But
when it comes to the Truth, what do the sacred scriptures say about it?
Let us ask you again and again where did you get the idea that Christ
was walking in the streets during what is known as the Stations of the
Cross with a cross on his back, and where does the teaching that he
fell three times under that cross come from? This teaching is believed
by most Christians and still also by many of those who usually read
the scriptures.

Allow us, with all the respect you deserve, to tell you that this
belief that we bring up that the Lord Jesus carried the cross is not
biblical, and for this justified reason, it is our responsibility to show
that the Lord Jesus never carried the cross. This is one of the many
still-existing traditions that have distorted the sheer reality of the
truth of the gospel of our Lord Jesus Christ. To bring you strong
evidence to demonstrate our position, below we will be presenting
articles as well as a few other comments from people who have tried

to present their views on this issue but, unfortunately, without any biblical basis.

Before going any further, let us present the list of the fourteen Stations of the Cross, also known as the Via Dolorosa or the Way of the Cross, which is a narrative of the final hours in the life of Jesus Christ on earth. There are several widely accepted versions that describe those final hours. One is biblical, and the others are rather traditional accounts of the events in Jesus's last hours. The traditional form of the Stations of the Cross or Via Crucis is as follows:

1. Jesus is condemned to death.
2. Jesus takes up his cross.
3. Jesus falls for the first time.
4. Jesus meets his mother Mary.
5. Simon of Cyrene is forced to carry the cross.
6. Veronica wipes the blood from Jesus's face.
7. Jesus falls the second time.
8. Jesus meets the women of Jerusalem.
9. Jesus falls the third time.
10. Jesus is stripped of his clothes.
11. Jesus is nailed to the cross—the Crucifixion.
12. Jesus dies on the cross.
13. The body of Jesus is removed from the cross—the Deposition or Lamentation.
14. The body of Jesus is placed in the tomb.

However, in the traditional way of the Cross, stations 3, 4, 6, 7, and 9 are not explicitly biblical. But this does not stop here. Let us continue to soak up the absolute truth that we are bringing up, hoping that we can be more grounded and obtain truthful knowledge of events based on scriptures and not on traditions.

There was a Catholic priest named Johannes Straubinger who, on page 306 of his article "Via Crucis," presents what is known as the fourteen stations, which consists of meditations. Before each of these fourteen stations that represent successive stages of the passion of our Lord, each station is marked by a small wooden cross that is usually found at the top of a painting relative to the subject of the meditation. In this article, Johannes Straubinger mentions some of the stations related to our topic under discussion. These are supposed stations on the route from the praetorium to Golgotha. Let's review.

1. Jesus is condemned to death.
2. Jesus carries the cross on his shoulders.
3. Jesus falls for the first time under the weight of the cross.
6. Veronica wipes the face of Jesus.
7. Jesus falls the second time to the ground.
9. Jesus falls to the ground for the third time.

Let us now note the irony of these stations that Johannes Straubinger presents on page 306 of his article on the way of the cross. He at no time pointed out where the passages or the biblical quotes for these stations were located. It is to wonder, Why did Mr. Straubinger not quote the passages for these stations? Actually, the answer is that there are no. The answer is simple. There is no passage in the Holy Scriptures to support these doctrinal points.

Let us look very carefully at what Mr. Straubinger says in the same article on the same page: "Several of these events are based on tradition and not on scripture, as for example, the case of Veronica."

It is necessary to note that the same Catholic dictionary gives us information from where this teaching originated, in the same article on the Via Crucis and by the same writer who wrote the following: "This devotion arose in the middle of the 15th century among the minor friars who practiced as a kind of spiritual pilgrimage to the holy places of Jerusalem that were under his custody [in addition]. In 1894, Innocent XII decreed that the indulgences that were earned by visiting the holy places could be earned by the minor friars and their affiliates who prayed at the Stations of the Cross."

As we can see, the same Catholic data affirms that it has been tradition that imposed what is related to the events of the Lord's passion. And from there arose the idea that Jesus carried the cross and that he fell three times to the ground, an idea that is promoted by most religions, except for, unfortunately, only a small part of our Christian churches of which we still do not dare to affirm which or who they are.

CHAPTER 14

KNOW THE TRUTH OUTSIDE
OF ROMAN MYTHS

Now let's take a close look at the Holy Scriptures, focusing on the holy gospels to get information of the truth regarding this matter so that we can clarify once and for all the interesting question whether Christ carried the cross or not. Well, starting from the premise that this is a very, very serious matter, let us use a little imagination. If Matthew were alive and we had the opportunity to ask him questions, we would ask him like this: Matthew, being the first witness who speaks in your book *Gospel According to Matthew*, from where to where did Christ carry the cross, and how many times did he fall carrying that very heavy cross? Now when we read Matthew 27:31–35, we find the answer that Matthew could have given us. Let's read: "After they had mocked him, they took off the robe and put his own clothes on him. Then they led him away to crucify him" (Matthew 27:31).

Crucifixion and death of Jesus

> As they were going out, they met a man from Cyrene, named Simon, and they forced him to carry the cross. They came to a place called Golgotha (which means "the place of the skull"). There they offered Jesus wine to drink, mixed with gall; but after tasting it, he refused to drink it. When they had crucified him, they divided

up his clothes by casting lots, so that what was
spoken by the prophet might be fulfilled: They
divided my clothes among themselves, and for
my clothes they cast lots. (Matthew 27:32–35)

Let us carefully analyze what Matthew tells us. Matthew practically tells us that after having mocked Christ, they took off his cloak and put his clothes on him. When they went outside to take him to be crucified, they found a man from Cyrene named Simon, and they forced him to carry the cross. And when they arrived at a place called Golgotha, which means "place of the skull," there they crucified him. Please, we hope that you will forgive us, but you don't have to be smart to understand that Simon carried the cross from the beginning when he left the praetorium to Golgotha to crucify the son of God on it.

On the other hand, note that Matthew at no time mentions that Christ carried the cross, but he also does not tell us that Simon helped him carry it. But rather he clearly tells us that Simon was forced to carry it. Nor does Matthew mention that Christ had fallen—not once, not three times, or at all (Judge for yourself, yes or no).

The second witness, Mark 15:20–21 states: "And when they had mocked him, they took off the purple robe and put his own clothes on him. Then they led him out to crucify him. [And he adds the story in its important part.] And they forced one who passed by, a certain man from Cyrene, Simon, the father of Alexander and Rufus, and was passing by on his way in from the country, and they forced him to carry the cross."

Another version reads like this: "When they finally got tired of making fun of him, they took off his purple robe and put his own clothes back on him. Then they took him away to crucify him. A man named Simon, who was passing by, but was from Cyrene, came from the field just at that moment, and the soldiers forced him to carry the cross of Jesus [Simon was the father of Alexander and Rufus]." Cyrene was a city in North Africa. This means that just when leaving that place of mockery, a character of African origin passed in front of the building, who was forced to carry the cross.

We believe that if Simon of Cyrene (the African) had known in advance that they would force him to carry the cross where Christ was going to be crucified on, to our understanding, he would have looked for another place to pass. In our country, it would have been said like this: "He would have taken the other way." Don't you think so? What would you have done? Note also that Simon did not help Christ at any time but was compelled.

The third witness is Lucas 23:25–26. The Gospel of Luke 1:1–4 says, "Many have undertaken to draw up an account of the things that have been fulfilled among us, just as they were handed down to us by those who from the first were eyewitnesses and servants of the word. With this in mind, since I myself have carefully investigated everything from the beginning, I too decided to write an orderly account for you, most excellent Theophilus, so that you may know the certainty of the things you have been taught."

I, too, have studied everything that happened very carefully, and I think it's convenient to put it in writing, just as it happened. This way, you will be able to know if they have told you the truth. In these verses, the responsibility of Luke stands out, to say that his writings are based on the truth and that he was writing as he received the news without adding to it and without adding gossip to it. He says, "I have studied very carefully what they have told me." And he refers to writing as it happened, because he mentions that some were already changing the real story about the events of the Lord Jesus and that this truth does not depend on traditions but on those who saw the facts of Jesus Christ with their eyes.

Therefore, the truth regarding this matter is found in the writings of these holy men, who were eyewitnesses of that martyrdom of Jesus, seen and written by his apostles and in some writings given by the prophets, where the suffering of the Lord is announced, such as what we have previously studied in the prophet Isaiah.

Of course, anyone can argue: What is wrong with it being said that Christ carried the cross? What wrong is being done? Or that this is of no importance. But Jesus was very clear about his holy word and said in the Gospel of John 17:17: "Your word is the truth, sanctify them in your truth." Translation in current language is as follows: "Your message is the truth; make that when listening to it, they give themselves totally to you."

Therefore, to say or teach what is not written is to contradict the Holy Spirit of God and Jesus Christ; there is no doubt.

If he says your word is true, he will not go halfway or be announced in a wrong way. There is, from that time then, a misrepresentation of that word. Let us review the holy gospels to obtain the truth of this matter.

In Matthew 27:31–32, it says, "After they had mocked him, they took off the robe and put his own clothes on him. Then they led him away to crucify him." The story is clear that if we go back to the last moments of the life of the Lord, the evangelist tells us that after the derision made of him, they went out to crucify him, and he adds, "As they were going out, they met a man from Cyrene, named Simon, and they forced him to carry the cross."

The following version reads: "And he released him who had been thrown into jail for sedition and a death for which they had asked, and he delivered Jesus to their will and taking him, they took a Cyrenean who came from the field and they put the cross on him so that he would carry it after Jesus."

In these three gospels, the harmony that exists in the same story can be noted that after he had been unjustly condemned and without proving anything worthy of death, he was taken to the place of the skull to be crucified. Yet the three witnesses are very clear that it was Simon of Cyrene who carried the cross behind Jesus, so it can be seen that Jesus did not carry the cross at any time.

In the Roman tradition, it is said that Simon helped him with the last cross, which means that, together, they carried the cross. But this is only a conjecture because the Holy Scriptures do not say anything about it. Nor do we find that Jesus has fallen three times under the heavy cross. And they believe that in one of his falls, he met Mary Magdalene and that when she wipes his face with a cloak, the wounded face of Jesus Christ is imprinted onto it; this is all a Roman myth and one that most Christians have believed to this day.

CHAPTER 15

APPARENT CONTRADICTION

Now we will analyze the writings of the evangelist John, undoubtedly the inventor of the tradition used to make the world believe that the Lord Jesus carried the cross. John is interested in everything spiritual and heavenly of Jesus Christ and not in the record of the facts.

Let's read then in John 19:16: "Finally Pilate handed him over to them to be crucified. So, the soldiers took charge of Jesus." The verse clearly says that Pilate gave him to them so that the people could crucify him, so the crowd took Jesus and carried him to the place of sacrifice. But what about the wooden cross? Obviously behind him was Simon of Cyrene with it, but in verse 17 is where there is some minor confusion because we read, "Carrying his own cross, he went out to the place of the Skull [which in Aramaic is called Golgotha]." But what cross was John referring to? Well, he was not referring to the wooden cross because in no way could he contradict his three companions—Matthew, Mark, and Luke—who were eyewitnesses that Jesus did not take the wooden cross to the place of the skull.

John was with the Lord most of the time, and when he says "Taking up his cross," he refers to the sacrifice of the Master that began from the moment they took him out of the court to crucify him. This was where he truly felt the anguish and his reverent submission. Thus, says the letter to Hebrews 5:7 during the days of Jesus's life on earth, he offered up prayers and petitions with fervent cries and tears to the one who could save him from death, and he was heard because of his reverent submission. And the night before, he had prayed, saying, "My Father, if it is possible, may this cup be taken from me. Yet not as I will, but as you will" (Matthew 26:39). And again, he said, "My soul is overwhelmed with sorrow to the point of death." All these fears and anguishes plus the lashes received previously were an affliction in the messiah, and above all, he felt the weight of the responsibility to his Father to redeem the world.

A day of pain awaited him until the time of his death. This was the crucial purpose for which the apostle John said, "Taking up his own cross." For these reasons stated, we are sure that none of the eyewitnesses, who are the four evangelists, could have been wrong. Now he also tells us, the children of God, to read well the following:

> Then Jesus said to his disciples, "Whoever wants to be my disciple must deny themselves and take up their cross and follow me." (Matthew 16:24)

> Then he called the crowd to him along with his disciples and said: "Whoever wants to be my disciple must deny themselves and take up their cross and follow me." (Mark 8:34)

> Then he said to them all: "Whoever wants to be my disciple must deny themselves and take up their cross daily and follow me." (Luke 9:23)

We ask ourselves, and we also ask you, Should we go buy or make a literal wooden cross for ourselves? Is it literal, or is it symbolic that you and I carry it because to the letter of the word, it is a condition—deny yourself, take up your cross, and follow me? We want you to analyze this important matter for our spiritual lives because it is very interesting, and it is necessary to understand the truth of God. This does not mean that we question our faith. On the contrary, each day, we will love our God more. Men write on paper, and God writes on our hearts. Read the Gospel of John 19:17–20, and you will understand more about Jesus:

Carrying his own cross, he went out to the place of the Skull (which in Aramaic is called Golgotha). There they crucified him, and with him two others—one on each side and Jesus in the middle. Pilate had a notice prepared and fastened to the cross. It read: Jesus of Nazareth, the king of the Jews. Many of the Jews read this sign, for the place where Jesus was crucified was near the city, and the sign was written in Aramaic, Latin and Greek.

Be careful. I hope you can realize this. When Matthew, Mark, and Luke referred to the cross that Simon carried from the praetorium to Calvary, they called it "the cross," which means that they spoke of a literal cross.

While John said, "And he, carrying his cross, reached Golgotha." Here, John is expressing himself spiritually, referring to the Calvary through which Christ was passing. That is why we point to the verses in which Jesus said, "Whoever wants to continue in peace with me, deny himself, take up his cross and follow me." Since Christ expressed himself this way, John, who was imitating him and who was writing to the church in a spiritual tone, was not referring to the cross but to the sacrifice that Christ was carrying.

CHAPTER 16

THE TRUE DAY AND TIME
CHRIST DIED

Hoping not to hurt any feelings, we cast these questions to all our potential readers: When did our Lord Jesus Christ really die? Would it be a Friday, or on what day exactly did Jesus die? Unfortunately, it is still the case, and we dare to express it this way that many historians and biblical scholars have not been able to and have not managed to agree on the matter.

Certainly, although the Christian tradition indicates that Jesus was crucified and that he died on a Friday, which has been called Good Friday, and although traditionally, Christian believers celebrate the crucifixion and death of Jesus on the well-known Good Friday of each year, also known as the time of Holy Week, implying that our Lord Jesus Christ died that day of the week, as far as we are concerned, we do not agree with these observations or rather the data and theories on these issues, from which we totally differ.

Now as our commitment is to reveal the hidden realities that exist around the crucifixion of Jesus Christ, we proceed to bring you hard data, which will make you think about and which we are sure will help you adopt your own conclusions and not conclusions such as, "I believe that...," "I imagine...," "They taught me that...," etc.

Well, actually, do you know what day Jesus died? Jesus died on a Friday, or when else? Let's go to the data and theories available, taking into account that in the gospels, it is not specifically mentioned what day of the week Jesus died after he was crucified on Mount

Calvary. This has led many to misinterpret and make countless erroneous deductions based on information found in biblical texts. This does not mean that the biblical texts are wrong. Will they be right or wrong?

Let's carefully analyze this important fact: the time that Jesus died. The Bible, according to the gospels, indicates that Jesus died at the ninth hour, understanding that they were referring to nine hours after sunrise, which is around three in the afternoon. According to the scripture, after Christ was already dead, the Jews, because it was during the preparation of the Passover and so that the bodies would not be left on the cross on the Sabbath (for that Sabbath was of great solemnity), begged Pilate that their legs be broken and that they be removed from there.

Then Joseph of Arimathea—who had been one of Jesus's disciples and who had a strong conviction that Jesus was the messiah but had, in turn, feared the consequences of publicly acknowledging his faith (John 19:38)—secretly went to Pilate and asked for the body of Jesus so that he could provide a proper burial. And after it was delivered to him, he immediately took the body of Christ down from the cross. Then he wrapped it in a cloth and proceeded to bury it that same night because it was the day of preparation or Sabbath, which is the eve of the Sabbath. To secure it, he put it in a tomb or sepulcher that was in a crag. Without wasting time, they rolled a very large stone in front of the tomb, sealing it to cover the entrance, before the astonished gaze of Mary, mother of Jesus, and Mary Magdalene.

We ask, What day of the preparation or Sabbath did the biblical texts refer to—the seventh day (Sabbath or Saturday) or another holy day? According to tradition, Jesus was crucified on a Friday afternoon and buried in a hurry on the night of the same Friday, since the next day, the Jews were to abstain from all activity, according to the fourth commandment. In this way, the prophecy that said that Christ would rise from the dead on the third day would be fulfilled. To which, obviously, we can observe that if Jesus was crucified on a Friday afternoon, dying that same Friday also in the same afternoon and resurrecting Sunday at dawn, we have to realize that Christ did not spend three full days buried, with twenty-four hours each, but spent part of Friday, Saturday or full Sabbath, and early Sunday morning, which, for the effects, were three days by name but not three twenty-four-hour days. We affirm, without fear of being wrong, that Jesus was crucified and that he died on a Wednesday instead of a Friday. Arguments from reliable sources claim that, in the week that Jesus died, there were two Sabbaths or days of rest: one on the day of the crucifixion, which may well have been the day of Pesach, which recalls the liberation of the Jewish people from slavery in Egypt, and another on the Saturday of that week.

Now, according to the Gospel of Mark, when the Sabbath passed, Mary Magdalene; Mary, the mother of James; and Salome bought aromatic spices to go and anoint the body of Christ. Judge for yourself. Women could not have bought such spices because they were not allowed to buy on that Sabbath. What do you think? Within this situation and considering the events that occurred between the death of Jesus and his resurrection on the first day of the week, which is on Sunday, the crucifixion and death had to have been obligatorily on Wednesday, the holy day. Pesach, it had to be Thursday. The women had to have bought the spices on Friday, then rested on Saturday or Sabbath as indicated by the Mosaic law, to finally discover that Jesus had risen on Sunday.

This point, the day that Jesus died, is important because most of us have been taught that he died on a Friday from where the so-called Good Friday comes, but we give all the honor and glory to God because he is who, through his Holy Spirit, lets us know in the scriptures these great truths. Are you reasoning? This question is still circulating in the air: On what day did Jesus Christ die?

Friday, the exclusive day of the time of the famous so-called Holy Week, marks the day of the death of our Lord Jesus Christ, and it is on that day that thousands and thousands of parishioners annually commemorate the death of Jesus. It would be healthy for us to take a look at this following passage: "He then began to teach them that the Son of Man must suffer many things and be rejected by the elders, the chief priests and the teachers of the law, and that he must be killed and after three days rise again" (Mark 8:31).

Note that Jesus said that, after three days of death, he was going to rise again, as he himself confirmed it many times. But let's not go too far yet. Let's also take another look at these following verses from the gospel according to Matthew 12:38–40.

> Then some of the Pharisees and teachers of the law said to him, "Teacher, we want to see a sign from you." He answered, "A wicked and adulterous generation asks for a sign! But none will be given it except the sign of the prophet Jonah. For as Jonah was three days and three nights in the belly of a huge fish, so the Son of Man will be three days and three nights in the heart of the earth."

These verses speak for themselves. Be careful. Based on what has been said previously, does it mean that Jesus rose again on a Tuesday instead of Sunday? Because if he died on Friday, then three days later, Tuesday comes to fall, which is in contradiction to the Sacred Scriptures that confirm and again confirm that Jesus rose on Sunday called Resurrection Sunday, which is what we all believe and therefore backed by the Bible.

We hope that we will not be misinterpreted. The Holy Scriptures are not those of errors; errors lie in the interpretations that can be given. Let us read Mark 16:9: "When Jesus rose early on the first day of the week, he appeared first to Mary Magdalene, out of whom he had driven seven demons." What is the first day of the week? Of course, it is Sunday, and the seventh day is Saturday, as it is written in Exodus 16:26, "Six days you are to gather it, but on the seventh day, the Sabbath, there will not be any."

In relation to this, it is clear to understand that a week has seven days, and if the seventh is Saturday, the first day of the week is Sunday. Let's read Mark 15:37, 42: "With a loud cry, Jesus breathed his last. It was Preparation Day [that is, the day before the Sabbath]. So as evening approached…" Here, the term *on the eve* can be used, which refers to the day that precedes and is immediately next to another day, especially if it is a holiday or special.

This indicates that it is from here that Jesus himself died Friday because if it was the eve of the Sabbath, and the Sabbath is Saturday. Then it is indisputable that he died on a Friday. Let's make well and very clear that when the Bible speaks of the Sabbath, we should not think precisely of Saturday because there are other Sabbaths that are not exactly Saturday. Let's read Leviticus 23:23–28:

> The Lord said to Moses, "Say to the Israelites: 'On the first day of the seventh month you are to have a day of sabbath rest, a sacred assembly commemorated with trumpet blasts. Do no regular work but present a food offering to the Lord.'" The Lord said to Moses, "The tenth day of this seventh month is the Day of Atonement. Hold a sacred assembly and deny yourselves and present a food offering to the Lord. Do not do any work on that day, because it is the Day of Atonement, when atonement is made for you before the Lord your God."

Let's take notice that it says that the first day is a Sabbath, and then it says that in the same month, the tenth day is also a Sabbath. Let's start from the premise that the first day was Saturday, then the day would be Monday, assuming that the day is Saturday. Let's remember well that when the Bible speaks of the Sabbath, it is not necessarily always referring to the Sabbath, unless it clearly says the seventh day. Let's make sure we understand this very clearly.

Let's read John 7:22: "Yet, because Moses gave you circumcision [though actually it did not come from Moses, but from the patriarchs], you circumcise a boy on the Sabbath." When was a man circumcised? It was done eight days after his birth, for it is written in Genesis 17:12: "For the generations to come every male among you who is eight days old must be circumcised, including those born in your household or bought with money from a foreigner—those who are not your offspring." That is why Jesus was circumcised eight days after his birth. Luke 2:21 states, "On the eighth day, when it was time to circumcise the child, he was named Jesus, the name the angel had given him before he was conceived." And we see that this day is declared a day of rest. Suppose that someone was born Tuesday. Eight days later, they circumcised him. That is, they would circumcise him on Tuesday, and that day for him and his parents was a day of rest. In conclusion, we reiterate that when the Bible says Sabbath, it can be any of the various Sabbaths unless it is said to be the seventh day.

CHAPTER 17

RELATION OF THE TIME OF PASSOVER TO THE DEATH OF CHRIST

Let me now introduce you to this other matter that is also very important to know regarding the time when Christ died. Jesus died during Passover, and it was customary to celebrate Passover in the month of Abib, which we know as April in our calendar. Let's read Numbers 28:16–25.

> On the fourteenth day of the first month the Lord's Passover is to be held. On the fifteenth day of this month there is to be a festival; for seven days eat bread made without yeast. On the first day hold a sacred assembly and do no regular work. Present to the Lord a food offering consisting of a burnt offering of two young bulls, one ram and seven male lambs a year old, all without defect. With each bull offer a grain offering of three-tenths of an ephah of the finest flour mixed with oil; with the ram, two-tenths; and with each of the seven lambs, one-tenth. Include one male goat as a sin offering to make atonement for you. Offer these in addition to the regular morning burnt offering. In this way present the food offering every day for seven days as an aroma pleasing to the Lord; it is to be offered in addition to the

regular burnt offering and its drink offering. On
the seventh day hold a sacred assembly and do no
regular work.

Let's observe that it says, "the first day." Suppose that the first
day fell on Saturday. The seventh day would be Friday, not Saturday,
but of the two days, both the first and the seventh are declared a
Sabbath because when saying "no servant work you will do," it refers
to those rest days. Let's read Leviticus 23:3: "There are six days when
you may work, but the seventh day is a day of sabbath rest, a day of
sacred assembly. You are not to do any work; wherever you live, it is
a sabbath to the Lord."

Again, this makes it clear to us that there were days other than
Saturday that were considered Sabbaths. Let's read John 19:31: "Now
it was the day of Preparation, and the next day was to be a special
Sabbath. Because the Jewish leaders did not want the bodies left on
the crosses during the Sabbath, they asked Pilate to have the legs
broken and the bodies taken down."

Therefore, it is clear that it was the eve of the Sabbath when
Jesus died, which is also clear that that Sabbath was of great solemnity. And this makes it clear once again that it was not an ordinary
Sabbath (i.e. Saturday), but it was one of the other Sabbaths that
were held in the Passover season, which was celebrated in the month
of April according to what is written in Exodus 12:1–2: "The Lord
said to Moses and Aaron in Egypt, 'This month is to be for you the
first month, the first month of your year.'"

We should give great importance to what follows as well, like
all the information that we consider of great interest and benefit,
which we are bringing to you. When the people of Israel left Egypt,
God established that the month in which they left would be the first
of the months of the year, but in what month did Israelites leave
Egypt? Let's read Exodus 13:3–4: "Then Moses said to the people,
'Commemorate this day, the day you came out of Egypt, out of the
land of slavery, because the Lord brought you out of it with a mighty

hand. Eat nothing containing yeast. Today, in the month of Abib, you are leaving.'"

Abib corresponds to the month of April, and it is in this month in which the Passover was celebrated. And in this month, there were several days of rest according to the above.

In conclusion, it is quite clear that Jesus rose from the dead on the first day of the week, Sunday, since it is written in Mark 16:9: "When Jesus rose early on the first day of the week." But if it was after three days, it means that Jesus died on a Wednesday.

Let us read again Mark 8:31: "He then began to teach them that the Son of Man must suffer many things and be rejected by the elders, the chief priests and the teachers of the law, and that he must be killed and after three days rise again."

CHAPTER 18

BOUGHT AT THE PRICE OF BLOOD

The death of Christ was a necessary punishment, which he bore for the sinner. Romans 4:25 states, "He was delivered over to death for our sins and was raised to life for our justification." 2 Corinthians 5:21 states, "God made him who had no sin to be sin[a] for us, so that in him we might become the righteousness of God." Galatians 1:4 states, "Who gave himself for our sins to rescue us from the present evil age, according to the will of our God and Father." Hebrews 9:28 states, "So Christ was sacrificed once to take away the sins of many; and he will appear a second time, not to bear sin, but to bring salvation to those who are waiting for him."

By paying the price of our ransom, Christ redeemed us. Three important Greek words are used in the New Testament to express this idea:

1. *Agorazo* means "to buy in a market." *Agora* means "market." Man, in his sin, is held under the sentence of death.

   Whoever believes in him is not condemned, but whoever does not believe stands condemned already because they have not believed in the name of God's one and only Son. (John 3:18–19)

   For the wages of sin is death, but the gift of God is eternal life in[a] Christ Jesus our Lord. A slave "sold under sin," but in the act of redemption he is bought by Christ through the shedding of his blood. (Romans 6:23)

We know that the law is spiritual; but I am unspiritual, sold as a slave to sin. (Romans 7:14)

You were bought at a price. Therefore, honor God with your bodies. (1 Corinthians 6:20)

You were bought at a price; do not become slaves of human beings. (Corinthians 7:23)

But there were also false prophets among the people, just as there will be false teachers among you. They will secretly introduce destructive heresies, even denying the sovereign Lord who bought them—bringing swift destruction on themselves. (Peter 2:1)

And they sang a new song, saying: "You are worthy to take the scroll and to open its seals because you were slain, and with your blood you purchased for God persons from every tribe and language and people and nation." (Revelation 5:9)

And they sang a new song before the throne and before the four living creatures and the elders. No one could learn the song except the 144,000 who had been redeemed from the earth. These are those who did not defile themselves with women, for they remained virgins. They follow the Lamb wherever he goes. They were purchased from among mankind and offered as first fruits to God and the Lamb. (Revelation 14:3–4:)

2. *Exagorazo* means "to buy and take off the sales market," which adds the thought not only of the purchase but also that it will never be for sale again, indicating that redemption is once and for all.

    Christ redeemed us from the curse of the law by becoming a curse for us, for it is written: "Cursed is everyone who is hung on a pole." (Galatians 3:13)

    To redeem those under the law, that we might receive adoption to sonship. (Galatians 4:5)

    Making the most of every opportunity, because the days are evil. (Ephesians 5:16)

    Be wise in the way you act toward outsiders; make the most of every opportunity. (Colossians 4:5)

3. *Lutroo* means "set free."

    But we had hoped that he was the one who was going to redeem Israel. And what is more, it is the third day since all this took place. (Luke 24:21)

    Who gave himself for us to redeem us from all wickedness and to purify for himself a people that are his very own, eager to do what is good. (Titus 2:14)

    For you know that it was not with perishable things such as silver or gold that you were redeemed from the empty way of life handed down to you from your ancestors. (1 Peter 1:18)

The same idea is found in the word *lutrosis.*

> Coming up to them at that very moment, she
> gave thanks to God and spoke about the child to
> all who were looking forward to the redemption
> of Jerusalem. (Luke 2:38)

> In a vision he has seen a man named Ananias
> come and place his hands on him to restore his
> sight. (Acts 9:12)

And there is another similar expression, *epoiesen lutrosin.* Luke
1:68 states, "Praise be to the Lord, the God of Israel, because he has
come to his people and redeemed them."

And there is another frequently used term, *apolutrosis*, indicating that a slave is freed.

> When these things begin to take place, stand up
> and lift up your heads, because your redemption
> is drawing near. (Luke 21:28)

> And all are justified freely by his grace through
> the redemption that came by Christ Jesus.
> (Romans 3:24)

> Not only so, but we ourselves, who have the first
> fruits of the Spirit, groan inwardly as we wait
> eagerly for our adoption to sonship, the redemp-
> tion of our bodies. (Romans 8:23)

> It is because of him that you are in Christ Jesus,
> who has become for us wisdom from God—that
> is, our righteousness, holiness and redemption.
> (1 Corinthians 1:30)

In him we have redemption through his blood, the forgiveness of sins, in accordance with the riches of God's grace, who is a deposit guaranteeing our inheritance until the redemption of those who are God's possession—to the praise of his glory. (Ephesians 1:7, 14)

And do not grieve the Holy Spirit of God, with whom you were sealed for the day of redemption. (Ephesians 4:30)

In whom we have redemption, the forgiveness of sins. But the Lord said to Ananias, "Go! This man is my chosen instrument to proclaim my name to the Gentiles and their kings and to the people of Israel." (Colossians 1:14)

Women received back their dead, raised to life again. There were others who were tortured, refusing to be released so that they might gain an even better resurrection. (Hebrews 11:35)

The concept of redemption includes buying, the prevention of selling, and complete freedom from individual redemption through the death of Christ and the application of redemption through the Holy Spirit.

So, too, the death of Christ was an offering, not like the animal offerings presented in the time of the Old Testament, which could only cover sin, in the sense of delaying the time of the just and deserved judgment against sin. In his sacrifice, Christ carried our sins with "his body on the tree," taking them away once and for all.

He was oppressed and afflicted, yet he did not open his mouth; he was led like a lamb to the slaughter, and as a sheep before its shearers is silent, so he did not open his mouth. By oppression and judgment he was taken away. Yet who of his generation protested? For he was cut off from the land of the living; for the transgression of my people he was punished. He was assigned a grave with the wicked, and with the rich in his death though he had done no violence, nor was any deceit in his mouth. Yet it was the Lord's will to crush him and cause him to suffer, and though the Lord makes his life an offering for sin, he will see his offspring and prolong his days, and the will of the Lord will prosper in his hand. After he has suffered, he will see the light of life and be satisfied; by his knowledge my righteous servant will justify many, and he will bear their iniquities. Therefore I will give him a portion among the great, and he will divide the spoils with the strong, because he poured out his life unto death, and was numbered with the transgressors. For he bore the sin of many and made intercession for the transgressors. (Isaiah 53:7–12)

The next day John saw Jesus coming toward him and said, "Look, the Lamb of God, who takes away the sin of the world!" (John 1:29)

Get rid of the old yeast, so that you may be a new unleavened batch—as you really are. For Christ, our Passover lamb, has been sacrificed. (1 Corinthians 5:7)

And walk in the way of love, just as Christ loved us and gave himself up for us as a fragrant offering and sacrifice to God. (Ephesians 5:2)

And find out what pleases the Lord. Have nothing to do with the fruitless deeds of darkness, but rather expose them. It is shameful even to mention what the disobedient do in secret. But everything exposed by the light becomes visible—and everything that is illuminated becomes a light. This is why it is said: "Wake up, sleeper, rise from the dead, and Christ will shine on you." (Ephesians 5:10–14)

Yet Saul grew more and more powerful and baffled the Jews living in Damascus by proving that Jesus is the Messiah. When he came to Jerusalem, he tried to join the disciples, but they were all afraid of him, not believing that he really was a disciple. (Acts 9:22, 26)

Otherwise, it would have been necessary for him to suffer many times from the beginning of the world but now, at the consummation of the ages, he submitted himself once and for all by the sacrifice of himself to put away sin. The death of Christ is represented on his part as an act of obedience to the law that sinners have broken, the act of which constitutes a propitiation or satisfaction of all the just demands of God on the sinner.

The Greek word *hilasterion* is used for the "propitiatory," which was the lid of the ark in the Most Holy place and which covered the law inside the ark. Hebrews 9:5 states, "Above the ark were the cherubim of the Glory, overshadowing the atonement cover." But we cannot discuss these things in detail now. On the Day of Atonement, the mercy seat was sprinkled with blood from the altar, and this changed the place of judgment into a place of mercy.

He is to take some of the bull's blood and with his finger sprinkle it on the front of the atonement cover; then he shall sprinkle some of it with his

finger seven times before the atonement cover.
(Leviticus 16:14)

But when Christ came as high priest of the
good things that are now already here, he went
through the greater and more perfect tabernacle
that is not made with human hands, that is to
say, is not a part of this creation. He did not enter
by means of the blood of goats and calves; but he
entered the Most Holy Place once for all by his
own blood, thus obtaining eternal redemption.
The blood of goats and bulls and the ashes of a
heifer sprinkled on those who are ceremonially
unclean sanctify them so that they are outwardly
clean. How much more, then, will the blood of
Christ, who through the eternal Spirit offered
himself unblemished to God, cleanse our con-
sciences from acts that lead to death, so that we
may serve the living God! For this reason Christ
is the mediator of a new covenant, that those
who are called may receive the promised eternal
inheritance—now that he has died as a ransom to
set them free from the sins committed under the
first covenant. (Hebrews 9:11–15)

Similarly, the throne of God becomes a throne of grace through
the propitiation of the death of Christ.

Therefore, since we have a great high priest who
has ascended into heaven, Jesus the Son of God,
let us hold firmly to the faith we profess. For we
do not have a high priest who is unable to empa-
thize with our weaknesses, but we have one who
has been tempted in every way, just as we are—
yet he did not sin. Let us then approach God's

throne of grace with confidence, so that we may receive mercy and find grace to help us in our time of need. (Acts 4:14–16)

A similar Greek word, *hilasmos*, refers to the act of propitiation; the meaning is that Christ, dying on the cross, fully satisfied all God's just demands regarding the judgment for humanity's sin.

He is the atoning sacrifice for our sins, and not only for ours but also for the sins of the whole world. (1 John 2:2)

This is love: not that we loved God, but that he loved us and sent his Son as an atoning sacrifice for our sins. (1 John 4:10)

God therefore declares that he forgives sins in his righteousness before the cross, on the basis that Christ would die and fully satisfy the law of justice.

God presented Christ as a sacrifice of atonement, through the shedding of his blood—to be received by faith. He did this to demonstrate his righteousness, because in his forbearance he had left the sins committed beforehand unpunished—he did it to demonstrate his righteousness at the present time, so as to be just and the one who justifies those who have faith in Jesus. (Romans 3:25–26)

In all this, God is described not as a God who delights in vengeance on the sinner but rather as a God who, out of his love, delights in mercy for the sinner. In redemption and propitiation, therefore, the believer in Christ is assured that the price has been paid in full, that they have been set free as a sinner, and that all of God's just demands for judgment upon them, because of their sins, have been satisfied.

Christ's death not only satisfied a holy God but provided the basis by which the world was reconciled to God. The Greek word *katallasso*, which means "to reconcile," has in itself the thought of bringing God and man together through a complete change in man. It appears frequently in various forms in the New Testament.

> For if, while we were God's enemies, we were rec-onciled to him through the death of his Son, how much more, having been reconciled, shall we be saved through his life! Not only is this so, but we also boast in God through our Lord Jesus Christ, through whom we have now received reconcilia-tion. (Romans 5:10–11)

> For if their rejection brought reconciliation to the world, what will their acceptance be but life from the dead? (Romans 11:15)

> But if she does, she must remain unmarried or else be reconciled to her husband. And a husband must not divorce his wife. (1 Corinthians 7:11)

> All this is from God, who reconciled us to him-self through Christ and gave us the ministry of reconciliation: that God was reconciling the world to himself in Christ, not counting peo-ple's sins against them. And he has committed to us the message of reconciliation. We are there-fore Christ's ambassadors, as though God were making his appeal through us. We implore you on Christ's behalf: Be reconciled to God. (2 Corinthians 5:18–20)

> And in one body to reconcile both of them to God through the cross, by which he put to death their hostility. (Ephesians 2:16)

> And through him to reconcile to himself all things, whether things on earth or things in heaven, by making peace through his blood, shed on the cross. Once you were alienated from God and were enemies in your minds because of your evil behavior. (Colossians 1:20–21)

The concept of reconciliation does not mean that God changes but that his relationship to man changes because of the redemptive work of Christ. Man is forgiven, justified, and spiritually resurrected to the level where he is reconciled to God. The thought is not that God is reconciled to the sinner, which is adjusted to a sinful state, but rather that the sinner is adjusted to the holy character of God. Reconciliation is for the whole world, since God redeemed the world and is the propitiation for the sins of the whole world.

> All this is from God, who reconciled us to himself through Christ and gave us the ministry of reconciliation: that God was reconciling the world to himself in Christ, not counting people's sins against them. And he has committed to us the message of reconciliation. (2 Corinthians 5:18–19)

> And in one body to reconcile both of them to God through the cross, by which he put to death their hostility. (Ephesians 2:16)

> Since you died with Christ to the elemental spiritual forces of this world, why, as though you still belonged to the world, do you submit to its rules:

"Do not handle! Do not taste! Do not touch!"?
(Colossians 2:20–21)

The death of Christ removed all moral impediments in the mind of God to save sinners who, from sin, have been redeemed through the death of Christ. God has been satisfied, and man has been reconciled to God. There is no more obstacle for God to freely accept and justify anyone who believes in Jesus Christ as his Savior.

Romans 3:26 states, "He did it to demonstrate his righteousness at the present time, so as to be just and the one who justifies those who have faith in Jesus." With the death of Christ, the infinite love and power of God are freed from all restrictions to save, as all the judgments that divine justice could demand against the sinner have been fulfilled in it. There is no one in the entire universe who has benefited more than God himself from the death of his beloved Son. In his death, Christ became the substitute who suffered the penalty or punishment that the sinner deserved.

> He is to lay both hands on the head of the live goat and confess over it all the wickedness and rebellion of the Israelites—all their sins—and put them on the goat's head. He shall send the goat away into the wilderness in the care of someone appointed for the task. (Leviticus 16:21)

> We all, like sheep, have gone astray, each of us has turned to our own way; and the Lord has laid on him the iniquity of us all. (Isaiah 53:6)

> It is written: "And he was numbered with the transgressors; and I tell you that this must be fulfilled in me. Yes, what is written about me is reaching its fulfillment." (Luke 22:37)

Just as the Son of Man did not come to be served, but to serve, and to give his life as a ransom for many. (Matthew 20:28)

I am the good shepherd. The good shepherd lays down his life for the sheep. (John 10:11)

You see, at just the right time, when we were still powerless, Christ died for the ungodly. Very rarely will anyone die for a righteous person, though for a good person someone might possibly dare to die. But God demonstrates his own love for us in this: While we were still sinners, Christ died for us. (Romans 5:6–8)

For Christ also suffered once for sins, the righteous for the unrighteous, to bring you to God. He was put to death in the body but made alive in the Spirit. (1 Peter 3:18)

This truth is the foundation of certainty for everyone who approaches God in search of salvation. Furthermore, this is a fact that each individual must believe concerning his own relationship with God, as it pertains to the problem of sin. Generally believing that Christ died for the world is not enough; a personal conviction is demanded from the scriptures that one's own sin was that which Christ, our substitute, completely bore on the cross. This is the faith that results in a sense of inner rest, inexplicable joy, and deep gratitude toward him.

May the God of hope fill you with all joy and peace as you trust in him, so that you may overflow with hope by the power of the Holy Spirit. (Romans 15:13)

> How much more, then, will the blood of Christ,
> who through the eternal Spirit offered himself
> unblemished to God, cleanse our consciences
> from acts that lead to death, so that we may serve
> the living God! (Hebrews 9:14)

> Otherwise, would they not have stopped being
> offered? For the worshipers would have been
> cleansed once for all and would no longer have
> felt guilty for their sins. (Hebrews 10:2)

Salvation is a mighty work of God, instantly accomplished in the one who believes in Jesus Christ.

Fallacies concerning the death of the Son

The death of Christ is often misinterpreted. Every Christian will do well to fully understand the fallacy of the erroneous teachings that are being widely propagated on this subject today:

1. The doctrine of substitution is claimed to be immoral because it is said God could not, acting in strict justice, place the sins of the guilty on an innocent victim. This teaching might merit more serious consideration if it could be proved that Christ was an unwilling victim, but, on the contrary, the Bible reveals that he was in complete agreement with the will of his Father and was driven by the same infinite love.

    > It was just before the Passover Festival. Jesus
    > knew that the hour had come for him to leave
    > this world and go to the Father. Having loved his
    > own who were in the world, he loved them to the
    > end. (John 13:1)

> Then I said, "Here I am—it is written about me in the scroll—I have come to do your will, my God." In the same way, in the inscrutable mystery of divinity, it was God who "was in Christ reconciling the world to himself." (Hebrews 10:7)

> That God was reconciling the world to himself in Christ, not counting people's sins against them. And he has committed to us the message of reconciliation. (1 Corinthians 5:19)

The death of Christ was far from being a moral imposition. It was God himself, the just judge, who, in an act of love and sacrifice of himself, suffered all the punishment that his own holiness demanded for the sinner.

2.   It is asserted that Christ died as a martyr and that the value of his death consists of his example of courage and loyalty to his convictions. It is enough to answer this erroneous affirmation that, being Christ, the lamb offered in sacrifice by God. His life was not snatched away by any man, but he put it off himself to take it again.

> No one takes it from me, but I lay it down of my own accord. I have authority to lay it down and authority to take it up again. This command I received from my Father. (John 10:18)

> This man was handed over to you by God's deliberate plan and foreknowledge; and you, with the help of wicked men, put him to death by nailing him to the cross. (Acts 2:23)

3.   Christ is said to have died to exert a certain influence on one's moral character. That is to say, men who contemplate

the extraordinary event of Calvary will be constrained to give up their sinful life because on the cross, the divine concept of sin is revealed with singular intensity. This theory, which has no foundation in Scripture, assumes that God is currently seeking the reformation of men, when in reality, the crucifixion was the basis for their regeneration.

CHAPTER 19

APPROPRIATE SATISFACTION

Why was the sacrifice of our Lord Jesus Christ needed to pay the offense to God caused by the sin of our first parents and by personal sins? Why did God need to "collect" that debt or "receive satisfaction" with the appropriate payment being the death of his own Son?

The death of Jesus, preceded and accompanied by so much violence, is always a source of very deep questions. We know it is a source of love, but we also wonder if there was no other way to show that love or to give that forgiveness or to restore fallen humanity. The apostle Paul himself tells us that the cross is a "scandal" for the Jews and a "foolishness" for the non-Jews, as if indicating that the forces of human intelligence will never fully understand the reason for this way of saving us.

Sometimes, one of the concepts that have been proposed to explain the mystery of the crucifixion is used with excessive preference: his death was a way of "paying" a debt. First of all, it must be borne in mind that this way of speaking is just one of the various explanations that have been given. It is neither the oldest nor probably the best. However, when this very interesting topic is approached, we must bear in mind that this divine plan of salvation through the death of the Savior had been announced earlier in scripture as a mystery of universal redemption, that is, of a ransom that frees men from slavery to sin (John 8:34–36).

The most amazing thing about this is that it finally connects the death of Jesus with three other things: the design of God the Father, the reality of our sins, and the reality of what is revealed in Scripture. In other words, in the death of Christ, there is a plan of God that was already expressed in Scripture. This means that the fundamental question is not "Who was Christ paying?" but "What is that design, that will of God, that passes through that dark event?

That is why we must ask ourselves what was accomplished or what was achieved with Christ's death, since evidently, his death was not useless or accidental or the result of circumstances of the proximate history of Judea in the first century. The death of Christ was a lesson, a sacrifice, a sign of love, and a new beginning in creation. It was a lesson in several ways. Nothing shows the gravity of sin so much as seeing its consequences appear. The tortures that Christ suffered clearly show where betrayals, lies, cowardice, pride, envy, and many more iniquities go.

Each wound on his body teaches us something. The virtues that Christ showed in his passion are the most necessary for human's personal and social life: charity, patience, forgiveness, humility, defending the truth, and preferring to receive evil instead of causing it. Christ taught us not only how to live but also, above all, how to die. No matter how hard the end of our existence is, we will always find comfort and much light in the way Jesus entered the greatest and most overwhelming drama that every human being can face—death.

His meekness, his trust in God the Father, his prayer, and his wonderful detachment from everything earthly did not cease to be an unrivaled teaching, which he could hardly have given us in any other way, if not by letting himself die. And the fact that his death was so terribly painful makes the teaching penetrate us more and also serve the whole world, since it is indisputable that we all have to die.

The death of Christ was, without a doubt, a sacrifice. At the Last Supper, he himself spoke of his body, which would be "given," and of his blood, which would be "shed." Thus, he showed that the sacrifice of the paschal lamb for the Israelites was now going to happen in a "new and eternal [definitive]" way.

Virtually the entire letter to the Hebrews describes the death of Christ by comparing it to the sacrifices offered by the priests in the temple in Jerusalem. The comparison shows that everything has been improved, to the point that the old must be seen as a "shadow" or "figure" of the new. See for example Hebrews 10:10. The Revelation describes Christ several times as "the slaughtered lamb," a very graphic way of referring to his sacrifice.

At the same time, this slain lamb is the one who, by virtue of his victory, has the authority to judge all powers, since the powers of this world were unable to recognize and defend the innocence of the most just among the just. Christ's death was a sign of love, as we have already pointed out. First of all, Christ himself said that "there is no greater love than to give life" (John 15:13). And it is so, because he who gave his life can no longer give more; he has given everything. The act of wanting to suffer everything so that we could be liberated is an act of great love, very pure in its intention, arduous in its execution, and very fertile in its fruit.

One experiences that love of Christ when one realizes that the prayer of Christ as he died was a prayer for you and for us, in short, for each and every one. We can all say what the apostle Paul said: "Christ loved me and gave himself up for me" (Galatians 2:20). The way to experience it is to thank him for having prayed for us and say to him, "I believe in the redeeming love that you shed along with your blood on the altar of crucifixion," or similar words. It is difficult to think that one could have that experience if Christ had only been a good teacher or a great preacher.

The wonderful thing is, to see that his works of love go far beyond what can be said in words. The very passion of Christ describes to us numerous expressions of love, such as when he healed the ear of the soldier who came to seize him in Gethsemane (John 18:10), when he prayed for those who were torturing him and asked God to forgive them (Luke 23:34), when he announced paradise to the repentant thief (Luke 23:43), and when he took sweet care of both his mother and his beloved disciple (John 19:26–27).

This kind of delicate and, at the same time, very strong gestures of love have immense power in the human soul, if one meditates on them well. And it is evident that what makes this love so eloquent is that it implies that one must respond with love to hatred, that is, loving when it is most difficult or when, in fact, it seems impossible to love.

Christ's death marks a new beginning

If the kingdom of sin had to end (and that's what it's all about when we talk about redemption or salvation), it was necessary to mark that end—the end of the tyranny of sin and Satan. Christ announced, "Now the prince of this world is going to be cast out" (John 12:31). Death marks an end, that is to say, the worst the enemy could do was try to destroy the purest innocence, the most evident holiness. At first glance, one would say that he succeeded, because Christ did indeed die, but since he died without sinning, and this is crucial, then the power of the enemy was actually mocked and overcome. Christ himself said shortly before he died, "Everything is finished" (John 19:20).

It is a phrase that indicates an end and therefore announces a new beginning. Nothing speaks of the end as clearly as death. There is no transit or change in life that can be compared to the definitive, totalizing, and irreversible fact of dying. The gospels show that death did not have the last word. On the contrary, the very dark background of death makes the most intense light of resurrection stand out to the maximum. When after so many injustices and cruelties that Christ suffered, he greets us on Easter Day saying, "Peace be with you." We know that we can trust that peace. The apostle Paul also says, "If through baptism we die with Christ, we are sure that we will also live with him." We know that Jesus Christ was resurrected and will never die again, since death no longer has power over him. When Jesus Christ died, sin lost its power over him forever. (Romans 6:8–10).

All this indicates that Christ's death brought us immense goodness, and therefore, it may seem absurd at first, it is actually the revelation of God's wisdom (see 1 Corinthians 1, 2). On that basis, we can look at the word *satisfaction*, that is, In what sense did Christ have to "pay" something? The idea to pay comes from a "debt," which in Greek is *ofeiléma*. This data is important because in the prayer of Jesus, the Lord's Prayer, we say exactly to God to free us from our *ofeilémata*, which can be translated as "our debts." But what is an *ofeiléma*? It is an unfulfilled obligation, an outstanding account, or a debt. The underlying idea is that an *ofeiléma* is an obstacle in the relationship between two people. An example that we can give, which has nothing to do with any money, is when there are two friends. Let's say, one of the two finds out that the other has been speaking ill of him. The two friends meet again. And each realizes that the other already knows, but no one talks about it. Obviously, they cannot be treated with the usual camaraderie and closeness because there is "something pending." There is *ofeiléma*.

If we now look at our relationship with God, we see that the great *ofeiléma* is sin. But it is not simply saying, "I sinned. And now God forgives me, and everything is settled." To remove an *ofeiléma* is to restore trust, joy, and the feeling that there is free and open communication. That mutual love flows naturally. Anyone who has gone through that experience of seeking or receiving reconciliation knows of this.

So when we speak of "paying" or "giving satisfaction," the underlying idea is this: "remove obstacles" or also, "open the way" so that the life of God can flow, that is, a life of grace between God and man. It is not exactly "to please" God because he was "very angry" but to remove by way of love what became an obstacle due to lack of love, that is, the deficiency in loving God, as he deserves to be loved. The "payment" of Christ was then above all that. With the only love with which he loves, the Father loved us; and with the love with which he obeyed the Father, he also sought that everything that prevented the fulfillment of that will in us was removed.

Why did Jesus have to come to this world to suffer and die crucified? The truth is that he must have had a powerful reason, since it is strange that a father was able to send his only son to sacrifice himself for us. Certainly, it had to be a very urgent and, at the same time, pressing situation, where there was no other alternative. As we know, the most unusual thing is that, in the entire history of humanity, he has been the only one innocent of all crime or sin! Yes, Christ died because of sin, but not his own. Such is the greatness of the redemptive sacrifice of our Lord Jesus Christ.

CHAPTER 20

THE CROSS AS A RELIGIOUS SYMBOL

The cross is a religious symbol, which has been well-known through-out the world and, in turn, more emblematic of Christianity. The cross represents, for many parishioners, one of the most transcendent events in history, namely, the sacrifice that Christ made voluntarily to save humanity. As a curious thing, many people, for many years, have been wearing a cross on their chest, according to them, as a pendant or ornament. And they are also used by churches. They are used in cemeteries, and there are those that are used linked in chains around the neck or on the wrists, despite the fact that, in the time of Jesus Christ, the cross was a symbol of shame and curse.

Let us read the epistle of Saint Paul the apostle to Galatians 3:13: "Christ redeemed us from the curse of the law by becoming a curse [for it is written: Cursed is everyone who is hung on a pole]." But with all that, for many, the cross remains the symbol of Christianity. Judge for yourself. Do you think that our churches should have a cross stamped at the entrance of the church and, many times, as an emblem on the pulpits? How should you feel when you are wearing a figure of a cross as an ornament or amulet, even more so knowing that it is a symbol of shame and curse?

It is necessary to know that, in the Bible, the instrument of execution that was used to crucify Christ is not described. To all this, that being so and that although there is little knowledge of what this instrument of execution was like, the Bible makes it clear to us that Jesus died crucified on a log.

Let's define this crucifixion issue. Crucifixion is the process by which a person is nailed or tied to a crossbeam or stake. According to existing information that emerges from reliable data, the crucifixion process was, at its beginnings, used by the Persians and then later by the Egyptians, then also by the Carthaginians and consequently by the Romans as a form of death penalty. It has been proven that Alexander the Great introduced it to the Mediterranean area, and the Romans adopted it as a means to punish some prisoners with death.

In many of the cases, they had a stake permanently on the ground, indicating the place where the sentenced person would be crucified and carrying themselves their own crossbeam to the place marked with the stake. The crossbeam part weighed about fifty to seventy-five pounds. Many times, the person was nailed to these crossbeams in the shape of a cross, and at other times, they were tied. Then regardless of the case, nailed or tied, these people were raised, nailed to the crossbeam, and placed in a notch that was in the upper part of the stake, wherever it was.

When these crossbeams were raised together with the victim, they gave the impression of a T. Another way used in those times was to place these transverse beams a few meters below the top, thus forming a cross. There was another way where a person was nailed or tied to an individual stake buried in the ground with a small wooden sign describing the crime committed by the sentenced person, which was brought before the victim, leading the procession to the place of execution, and then placed on the pole, where he was to be executed, above his head.

We want to continue adding more truthful and, at the same time, reliable information regarding the way in which Jesus was crucified. Through the gospels, we know that Christ was crucified, and when it is said that Jesus was crucified, it should be understood that he was not tied but was nailed to the cross-shaped stake. Let's read, "When they came to the place of the skull, they crucified him" (John 19:17–18).

By way of clarification, for the Romans, the wrist is considered part of the hand where nails were used. These were nailed through the wrists, which passed through the wrists between the bones and not through the palms of the hands. And this is due to the fact that the nail could very well tear the palm of the hand, thus not being able to support the entire weight of the body. It is known that Jesus was nailed by the wrist to prevent the nails from coming out of his hands with the weight of his body. The executioners who were used for these executions were fully trained, so when they pierced the wrists, they did not break any bones. And due to their experiences, they inserted the nails through the most appropriate and exact place so that the body was well supported.

The scriptures say so. "None of his bones will be broken" (Psalm 34:20 and John 19:36). Such was the accuracy of these soldiers that they did not pierce any of the important arteries, because if this had happened, Christ would have bled out immediately. Truly, the Roman executioners were expert professionals; there is no doubt. Well, we cannot fail to mention the method they used for the feet, since once the hands were nailed, the feet had to be nailed. And for that, they needed two or more soldiers who would take the cross-beam with Christ nailed to it and lift them, raising it to the height where the horizontal beam will be fixed to the post or (vertical pole).

After this, they proceeded to nail the feet, which, when done in this way, made the task relatively easier for them. Once the horizontal beam was fixed on the vertical pole (post), they crossed their thighs and legs, bent their knees slightly upwards at an angle of about 120 degrees, and put one foot on the other. They nailed them to the pole, making sure not to stretch the legs or feet too low. If not, then Jesus could not have moved, having as the only point of support was the nail nailed through his feet.

It, too, was necessary for Christ to have the opportunity to move so that he could move upward with his body, which would let him breathe and expel the stale air at the same time. Had it not been so, Christ would have died quickly by suffocation. Now then, we want to point out, being sure of this, that three nails were used to crucify Christ—one in each of the wrists and the other in the feet. I hope you have noticed that we have mentioned that three nails were used to crucify Christ. If perhaps there would be an additional fourth nail, it was not to nail the body of Christ but to nail the little wooden sign, which was used in, some cases, describing the crime committed by the sentenced person or something related to the victim.

We hope that this is very clear. Once again, the veracity of the Holy Scriptures was verified, because here, this part of the scripture had been fulfilled: "They have pierced my hands and my feet" (Psalm 22:16). There are those who affirm that, in the post or (vertical pole), there was a kind of seat, that is, Christ was placed on a suppedaneum. It is a platform to support the feet called sedile so that Christ could rest his body, since, due to the law of gravity, his body would tend to sag.

From one point of view, that could have happened, but in the case of Jesus, the vertical pole in which Christ was crucified did not have it for the reason that it was only used in some provinces of the empire with people who had committed acts highly unforgivable through their misdeeds or betrayals to which they wanted to lengthen the torment, prolonging the suffering and agony.

CHAPTER 21

SYMBOL OF SHAME AND CURSES

Although no one knows exactly when Christendom assumed the cross as its proper symbol, the cited *Vine Dictionary* states, "In the middle of the 3rd century A.D., the Churches had departed from certain doctrines of the Christian faith or had perverted them. In order to increase the prestige of the apostate ecclesiastical system, pagans were welcomed into the churches apart from regeneration by faith and were allowed to in large maintain their signs and symbols. Hence the cross was adopted."

There are writers who point to an event from the year 312 of our era. They say that the emperor Constantine, who worshipped the sun, claimed to have had a vision during one of his military campaigns in which he contemplated a cross on the astral king along with the Latin words *In hoc vince*, which means "with this, he conquers." Later, the banners, shields, and armor of his army displayed a "Christian" sign (pictured on the left). According to the accounts, Constantine became a Christian, although he did not receive baptism until twenty-five years later on his deathbed. And some scholars question his motives. For example, a certain literary work states, "With his conduct he implied that his main interest was not so much to embrace the teachings of Jesus of Nazareth, as to convert Christianity into a Catholic religion [or universal] that would be easy for his subjects to accept" (*The Non-Christian Cross*). Since then, crosses of all kinds have been used. Among others, the *New Certeza*

Biblical Dictionary mentions the so-called "cross of Saint Anthony" with "the shape of a capital T, which some believe is derived from the symbol of the [Babylonian] god Tammuz," namely the letter tau. This dictionary also refers to the cross of St. Andrew, shaped like the letter X, and the familiar two-bar cross with the lowest horizontal. On the latter, known as Latin, he adds, "The tradition [that] was the cross on which our Lord died" maintains. As we have seen, that tradition is without foundation.

What did first-century Christians believe? The Bible shows that, in the first century, there were many people who heard what Christ taught, believed in him, and accepted the redemptive value of his death. Years later, when Paul preached to the Jews in Corinth, he showed them that Jesus was the messiah. As a consequence, "Crispus, the synagogue leader, and his entire household believed in the Lord; and many of the Corinthians who heard Paul believed and were baptized" (Acts 18:5–8). Far from recommending that they use some new symbol or image in worship, the apostle exhorted them: "Flee from idolatry" (1 Corinthians 10:14).

Logically, this included all practices of pagan origin. No historian or researcher has found strong evidence that the early Christians used the cross. Furthermore, this other point made by a late-seventeenth-century writer (as quoted in the *History of the Cross*) is interesting: "When Jesus sees his disciples expressing pride in the image of the [supposed] instrument of execution where, despising the shame, he suffered suffering despite being innocent. Could he possibly feel pleased?" What do you think?

The worship that God accepts does not need images or any other object. In fact, Paul asked, "And what agreement does God's temple have with idols?" (2 Corinthians 6:14–16). There is not a single passage in scripture that even implies that Christians must use in worship a representation of the instrument of torture where Jesus died (compare Matthew 15:3 and Mark 7:13).

So what is the identifying mark of true Christians? It is neither the cross nor any other symbol; it is love. Christ himself indicated this when he told his followers: "A new command I give you: Love one another. As I have loved you, so you must love one another. By this everyone will know that you are my disciples, if you love one another" (John 13:34–35).

CHAPTER 22

WHAT HAPPENED TO THE NAILS THAT WERE USED TO CRUCIFY CHRIST?

The story of the nails used to crucify Christ is followed today by a legend and even a bit of mystery. At present, these nails have an interesting history that even today, to our understanding, is discussed very, very little and that we will try to explain to you. We ask ourselves, Where have these nails gone? According to the following story, in the fourth century AD and during the reign of Emperor Constantine I, the area of Mount Golgotha was excavated, giving the opportunity to find the so-called true cross, that is, the true cross of Christ, whose nails were still embedded in. It is said that before this finding, the mother of said emperor, named Helena, had two of the nails melted—one of them to be included in her son's breastplate, and with the second, she devised a bit for the horse used by her son, believing that, with this, his son would have divine protection bestowed upon him by God in his future battles.

On the other hand, it is said that one of the other nails melted down then cast and included in the so-called iron crown, which was used for the coronation ceremony of the kings of Italy around the Middle Ages. For this purpose, this next nail was cast to give it the shape of a circular sheet of iron that was incorporated into the crown on the inside. An effect was that, during the Middle Ages, the territory of Italy became part of the Holy Roman Empire whose best-known emperor in the high Middle Ages was Charlemagne. The emperors of the Holy Empire were crowned three times: once as king of Italy, once as king of Germany, and once as emperor.

In 775, Charlemagne was crowned with this iron crown, which, for some, could be another reason for the legendary semidivine status of this emperor. At the beginning of the nineteenth century, another great character in our history was associated to the iron crown, and we refer to Napoleon Bonaparte, who proclaimed himself on that occasion king of Italy. Today these relics are venerated in different places, as the iron crown is preserved in the old cathedral of Monza, the former capital of Lombardy.

We do not want to stop pointing out that, in Rome, some architects and bricklayers built a basilica dedicated to the so-called holy cross, where this relic is still venerated today along with a fragment of the sign of the cross. Also, on the other hand, the Church of the Holy Sepulcher (in Jerusalem) was built on Mount Golgotha, the place where Christ was crucified, also having the purpose of showing exactly where Jesus died. But let us bring you another matter of utmost importance, which is that the first Christians could not publicly adopt the symbol of the cross since this would expose them to danger. In fact, the cross did not spread until the arrival of Constantine in the fourth century. He is, being the emperor, who established religious tolerance toward Christians. The images that were worshipped at that time among Christians were very diverse. In particular, they used the symbols of the fish, the bread, the dove, and even different types of crosses.

As we have previously pointed out, the cross is the main symbol of Christianity, referring to all those different Christian communities that venerate the cross. The form of each one of them varies from one to the other between these different Christian communities. For example, not to mention some, the cross of the Catholic Church is a vertical line crossed in its upper part by a horizontal line known as the Latin cross. Within the Orthodox Church, the eight-armed cross predominates.

It is necessary to let you know that, although the cross is one of the greatest symbols in the history of humanity, this venerable sign, which is a symbol of the Christian world, was not born with Christ, since it has a long history that goes back to six thousand years before the birth of Jesus. Pay attention to this. Through a note found in the literary work *Universal History of the Catholic Church*, whose author is René F. Rohrbacher, it is clearly explained that this term of the cross as well as its equivalent in Hebrew "do not really mean what we understand by cross, but rather that it is a simple log." It is necessary now, if it has not been done yet, to raise awareness and analyze. Is it correct to worship a cross like praying to a crucifix?

It is very sad and seriously regrettable to know that, at this point in life, there are many parishioners who have the mentality of praying to a cross or crucifix. They even practice making the sign of the cross without knowing that this act is not pleasing to God. By the way, did you know that the sign of the cross is not the same for all Christians who usually venerate the cross? For example, this ritual is carried out with a different hand position between Catholics and Orthodox. Furthermore, the latter first touch the right shoulder, and then the left.

Well, let's talk about the crucifix. Apparently, this name is like a composition of two parts, cross and fixed. This, without a doubt, literally means "fixed to the cross." Through the crucifix, an attempt is made to graphically represent the palpable suffering of Jesus's sacrifice, in other words, of his crucifixion.

The crucifix first appeared in the tenth century. It was first used occasionally, and then its popularity increased to such an extent that the crucifix became part of the Christian liturgy, although its veneration in the Protestant Church is less and, even in many, is unacceptable. It is obvious that for those different Christian communities that venerate the cross, the difference between the cross and crucifix is remarkable in that the crucifix is much more pronounced. And it is precisely due to the accuracy of the image that this last symbol provokes that makes some of the faithful feel better identified with the figure of Christ.

CHAPTER 23

NEW YEAR'S CELEBRATION

We have touched on the themes of the birth of Jesus, his death, etc. But it would be good to touch, even briefly, the theme of the New Year, which is celebrated every year. According to many historical researchers, the New Year's celebration dates back four thousand years, but it did not begin in Western cultures until just four hundred years ago. This tradition began in ancient Babylon (now Iraq) around 2000 BC. However, the Babylonians began their New Year near the end of what is now March, a logical time to start a new year since winter had ended; spring, with its new life, began; and crops were planted for the next year.

In the year AD 153, how and when does the biblical year begin? The Romans start the year in January, in the middle of winter, while the Orthodox Jews start it in September to October, according to the commandments of their "rabbinic" leaders. Now we ask you and leave this question as an assignment: When is it, in our times, that we have to say goodbye to the old year and then receive the New Year?

CHAPTER 24

THE SECOND COMING OF CHRIST

It is established that the second coming of Christ is the event following the tribulation and that it is different from the rapture of the church. In the rapture, the Lord will come for his own just to take the church with him, while at the second coming, he will come accompanied by the church to carry out his judgments. Let's keep in mind and be very clear that the rapture will happen just before the tribulation begins, and the second coming of Christ will happen just after the tribulation ends. As a note of clarification, the second coming of Christ is the event that marks the end of the tribulation and thus the beginning of the great tribulation. Now let us point out an important detail of the second coming, which was prophesied in the Old Testament.

> A day of the Lord is coming, Jerusalem, when your possessions will be plundered and divided up within your very walls. I will gather all the nations to Jerusalem to fight against it; the city will be captured, the houses ransacked, and the women raped. Half of the city will go into exile, but the rest of the people will not be taken from the city. Then the Lord will go out and fight against those nations, as he fights on a day of battle. On that day his feet will stand on the Mount of Olives, east of Jerusalem, and the Mount of

Olives will be split in two from east to west, forming a great valley, with half of the mountain moving north and half moving south. You will flee by my mountain valley, for it will extend to Azel. You will flee as you fled from the earthquake [a] in the days of Uzziah king of Judah. Then the Lord my God will come, and all the holy ones with him. On that day there will be neither sunlight nor cold, frosty darkness. It will be a unique day—a day known only to the Lord—with no distinction between day and night. When evening comes, there will be light. On that day living water will flow out from Jerusalem, half of it east to the Dead Sea and half of it west to the Mediterranean Sea, in summer and in winter. The Lord will be king over the whole earth. On that day there will be one Lord, and his name the only name. (Zechariah 14:1–9)

This important prophecy begins by affirming that the day of Jehovah is coming. Jehovah's day refers to future events, some of which we have already studied. One of those events is the tribulation, and another is the second coming of Christ. Then before the second coming of Christ, there will be a military deployment in Israel and its capital, Jerusalem. It refers to the military campaign whose last battle is Armageddon. By the time this battle takes place, all the armies of the nations of the world will be held in Israel and more precisely in Jerusalem.

The city of Jerusalem will be taken. Its houses will be ransacked. Its women will be raped. And half of the population of Jerusalem will go into captivity, but the other half of the population will remain in the city. In the midst of this desolation, Jehovah will enter the battle and fight against those nations. It is interesting that if we make a comparison of this text with what we find in the book of Revelation 19:11–16, Jehovah is nothing more and nothing less than Jesus

Christ, the Son of man, that God-man who came to this earth for the first time to die on the cross for the sinner and who, after being entombed, rose again the third day and was ascended to glory, where he is, at this moment, with his glorified body waiting for his Father to make his enemies his footstool.

Zechariah is prophesying the time of his return to earth. He says that his feet will be established on that day on the Mount of Olives. This is the mountain from which the Lord departed in his first coming. As the disciples watched him get lost in the clouds, the angels that appeared after said, "Men of Galilee, why are you looking at the sky? This same Jesus who has been taken from you to heaven will come as you have seen him go to heaven."

Therefore, his coming must be at the Mount of Olives, and the Old Testament prophecy confirms this. The Mount of Olives will then split in the middle, making a very large valley, and half of the mountain will move toward the north and the other half toward the south. This, of course, means a total convulsion in the earth's crust. We saw this when we studied the battle of Armageddon.

Revelation 16:18 says, "Then there came flashes of lightning, rumblings, peals of thunder and a severe earthquake. No earthquake like it has ever occurred since mankind has been on earth, so tremendous was the quake." The witnesses to these events will be so scared that they will flee into the valley of the mountains. It is Jehovah or Jesus Christ coming with all who are his. It will be a known day of Jehovah, which will be neither day nor night, but when evening falls, there will be light because the one who is the light will already be on the earth. Jerusalem will be transformed, and living waters will come out of it because that is where Jesus Christ will be reigning, who is the living water.

Half of those waters will flow to the Eastern Sea or the Dead Sea, and the other half, to the Western Sea or the Mediterranean Sea, both in summer and winter, which indicates that all nature will have to be transformed. What has happened is that now Jesus Christ is controlling her. Jehovah or Jesus Christ will then be king over all the earth. All this has been prophesied by Zechariah, an Old Testament prophet, in approximately 520 BC. For Jehovah came in the person of Jesus, he was born of a virgin in an extremely humble place. There was no war, nor was the day darkened, and nor was the Mount of Olives split.

None of these things prophesied have come to pass, but this is because Zechariah's prophecy was not speaking of the first coming of Jehovah but of his second coming. Everything that Zechariah prophesied awaits fulfillment and will occur when the Lord Jesus Christ comes for the second time. We are left with this conclusion: the Old Testament prophesizes a second coming of Jehovah or Jesus Christ.

CHAPTER 25

DEBT SETTLED

We hope that these pieces of advice will not be forgotten, since sin damages our intimate relationship with God, but we want you to be very clear about this and to be able to understand it without getting into confusion. And it is that when a Christian sins, his situation or his legal position before God does not change in the least. He is still forgiven because "there is no longer any condemnation for those who are united to Christ Jesus" (Romans 8:8).

Salvation is not based on our merits but on God's free gift (Romans 6:23), and Christ's death certainly paid for all our sins: past, present, and future. Christ died for our sins (1 Corinthians 15:3) without any distinction. In theological terms, we continue to preserve our "justification." We remain children of God, and we still have membership in God's family. Our previous legal situation does not change.

> If we claim to be without sin, we deceive ourselves and the truth is not in us. (1 John 1:8)

> Dear friends, now we are children of God, and what we will be has not yet been made known. But we know that when Christ appears, we shall be like him, for we shall see him as he is. (1 John 3:2)

In theological terms, we continue to preserve our "adoption." Our fellowship with God is disrupted, and our Christian life is damaged. When we sin, God does not stop loving us, but he is displeased with us. When we disobey, God the Father is saddened. In Revelation 3, the risen Christ speaks from heaven to the church in Laodicea saying, "I rebuke and disciplined everyone I love. Therefore, be fervent and repent" (Revelation 3:19). The New Testament testifies to the displeasure of the three members of the trinity when Christians sin. See Isaiah 59:1–2 and 1 John 3:21.

The scriptures show that God's parental displeasure often leads to discipline in our Christian life. Hebrews 12:10 states, "They disciplined us for a little while as they thought best; but God disciplines us for our good, in order that we may share in his holiness." Regarding the need for a confession of sins, Jesus reminds us that we must pray every day: "Our debts being forgiven, as we also have forgiven our debtors" (Matthew 6:12; 1 John 1:9). When we sin as a Christian, it is not only our personal relationship with God that is disturbed but also our life and fruitfulness of ministry are also damaged.

John 15:4 states, "Remain in me, as I also remain in you. No branch can bear fruit by itself; it must remain in the vine. Neither can you bear fruit unless you remain in me." New Testament writers speak frequently of the destructive consequences of sin in the lives of believers. Paul says that when Christians yield to sin, they progressively become "slaves" of sin (Romans 6:16), while God wants Christians to continually grow in life the way of justice.

To sin is to go in the opposite direction and to move away from the likeness of God. It is to go in the direction that "leads to death" (Romans 6:16) and to eternal separation from God, a direction from which we were rescued when we became Christians. When we sin as Christians, we suffer a loss of heavenly reward.

Paul realizes that "it is necessary for all of us to appear before the judgment seat of Christ, so that each one receives what is due to him, according to the good or the bad that he has done while he lived in the body" (2 Corinthians 5:10). Paul implies that there are degrees of rewards in heaven and that sin has negative consequences in terms of loss of heavenly reward.

What is the unforgivable sin? Jesus says, "And so I tell you, every kind of sin and slander can be forgiven, but blasphemy against the Spirit will not be forgiven. Anyone who speaks a word against the Son of Man will be forgiven, but anyone who speaks against the Holy Spirit will not be forgiven, either in this age or in the age to come" (Matthew 12:31–32).

Jesus says in Mark 3:29–30, "But whoever blasphemes against the Holy Spirit will never be forgiven; they are guilty of an eternal sin." He said this because they were saying, "He has an impure spirit" (Mark 3:29; Luke 12:10). Likewise, Hebrews 6 says,

> It is impossible for those who have once been enlightened, who have tasted the heavenly gift, who have shared in the Holy Spirit, who have tasted the goodness of the word of God and the powers of the coming age and who have fallen away, to be brought back to repentance. To their loss, they are crucifying the Son of God all over again and subjecting him to public disgrace. (Hebrews 6:4–6) (compare with 10:26–27)

There are several interpretations on how to understand this sin of blasphemy against the Spirit: Some have thought that this was a sin that could only be committed while Christ was on earth. Jesus's statement in Matthew 12:31, "All sin and blasphemy may be forgiven" is so general that it seems unjustified to say that it refers only to something that could happen during his life, and the texts in question do not specify such restriction.

Some have held that this is a sin of unbelief that continues until death; therefore, everyone who dies in unbelief (or at least everyone who has heard Christ and dies in unbelief) has committed this sin. Upon reading these verses carefully, the explanation does not seem to fit the language of the quoted texts: "Why do these speak not of unbelief in general, but specifically of someone who speaks against the Holy Spirit?" (Matthew 12:32). It speaks of someone "that blasphemes against the Holy Spirit" (Mark 3:29) or "have turned away" (Hebrews 6:6).

Others hold that this sin is a serious apostasy of true believers and that only those who are truly born again can commit this sin. They base their interpretation on their understanding of the nature of "apostasy," which is mentioned in Hebrews 6:4–6 (which is the rejection of Christ by a true Christian and the consequent loss of salvation). But this does not seem to be the best understanding of Hebrews 6:4–6. Moreover, although this interpretation could perhaps be held with respect to Hebrews 6, it does not explain the blasphemy against the Holy Spirit in the passages of the gospels to which Jesus is responding to the insensitive denial of the Pharisees of the work of the Holy Spirit through him. A fourth possibility is that this sin consists in the willful, highly malicious, and slanderous rejection of the Holy Spirit's work of witness to Christ and attributing his work to Satan.

A more detailed message from the statement of Jesus, Matthew, and Mark shows that Jesus was speaking in response to the accusation of the Pharisees that "he does not cast out demons except through Beelzebub the prince of demons." The Lord had just healed a demon-possessed man who was blind and mute (Matthew 12:22). The Pharisees, despite these clear demonstrations of the Spirit's work in front of their eyes, deliberately rejected the authority of Jesus and his teachings and attributed them to the devil.

Jesus clearly told them that he knew their thoughts and said to them, "Every kingdom divided against itself will be ruined, and every city or household divided against itself will not stand. If Satan drives out Satan, he is divided against himself. How then can his kingdom stand?" (Matthew 12:25–26). So it was irrational and foolish for the Pharisees to attribute the miracles of Jesus to the power of Satan.

Matthew 12:28 states, "But if it is by the Spirit of God that I drive out demons, then the kingdom of God has come upon you." Matthew 12:30 states, "Whoever is not with me is against me, and whoever does not gather with me scatters." He warns that there is no neutrality, and certainly those who, like the Pharisees, oppose his message are against him. This sin consists in the willful, highly malicious, and slanderous rejection of the Holy Spirit's work of witness to Christ and attributing his work to Satan.

The deliberate and malicious defamation of the work of the Holy Spirit through Jesus, which the Pharisees attributed to Satan, would not be forgiven. The context indicates that Jesus is speaking of a sin that is not simply unbelief or rejection of Christ but includes: (1) a clear knowledge of who Christ is and the power of the Holy Spirit working through him, (2) a deliberate rejection of facts about Christ that his opponents knew to be true, and (3) maliciously ascribing the work of the Holy Spirit in Christ to the power of Satan.

In such a case, the hardness of the heart would be so great that the ordinary means of leading a sinner to repentance would have already been rejected. In this situation, it is not that the sin itself was so horrible that it could not be covered by the redemptive work of Christ, but rather that the sinner had so hardened his heart that it was already beyond God's ordinary means to offer forgiveness through repentance and Christ's confidence in salvation.

This sin is unforgivable because it isolates the sinner from repentance and saving faith by believing in the truth. There are those who wisely define this sin as follows: the fact that the unforgivable sin involves such a great hardening of the heart and lack of repentance indicates that those who fear they have committed sin but have sadness in their hearts for having sinned and wish to seek God certainly don't fall into the same category as those who are guilty of committing the unforgiveable sin. It is also said, "We can be reasonably sure that those who fear having committed it and worry about it and seek the prayers of others have not committed it."

CHAPTER 26

CHARACTERISTICS OF THE HUMAN BEING

Moses, when writing the history of creation, included two stories about the creation of the human being that might seem contradictory, but in reality, they come to be complementary to each other, because if we pay attention, they are talking about the same stories but from different perspectives. In the first story, Moses presents God's plan for man (Genesis 1:26–29), where God tells us that he created man in his own image and after his likeness and that he created male and female. That he not only created them in his image according to his likeness but also made them the dominator of nature and sexual beings, provided with food.

In the second account of the creation of human beings, note that the creation of man is totally different from the rest created by God. In the beginning, God created the heavens and the earth, by the single word (Genesis 2:7). Then the Lord God formed man from the dust of the ground and breathed into his nostrils the breath of life; and man was a living being. God, with his hands, formed the human being and said, "It is not good for the man to be alone. I will make a helper suitable for him." Here Moses reflects that the human being is not a lonely being but rather a social being and that both men and women need help.

For this purpose, God caused a deep sleep to fall on Adam. God took one of his ribs, and from the rib, he formed a woman and brought her to man so that they would be one flesh. We believe that

Moses, in these two stories about the creation of the human being, was directed by the Holy Spirit to affirm the position of creationism, which maintains that the human being is God's creation as expressed in the Holy Scriptures.

Now as God's creation, we are similar to him in many ways. We must firmly believe what the Bible says in Genesis, that God created man in his image and likeness and that male and female were created unlike the rest of creation, being an intelligent being with special characteristics created to be a steward of the environment. Being that God is not an indefinite impersonal being and that each person of the Trinity has personality and individuality, the human being also has personality and individuality just as God has it.

On the other hand, the terms *image* as well as *similarity* have the following meanings: the word *image* refers to the image produced by the shadow of a silhouette by the effect of the sun, and *similarity*, according to this term, the human being is not equal to God but similar. That is, it reflects some qualities of God but is not the same and is also not different; it is similar. We have much in common with the rest of creation, yet man is separated from the rest of creation because only man is made in the image of God. The Bible does not show that God has the form of a human being but that man has the form of God, in the use of intelligence, which is also a distinctive aspect of the human being.

When Adam and Eve were created, they were taught worship of the God of creation. We were created with conditional immortality. God is immortal. By creating the human being, he gave him the opportunity to be immortal like him, but the immortality he gave us was conditional. This depended on the decision that the human being made. Enjoying said immortality was conditional on obedience. Like God, the human being had the ability to act freely. We are more than sure that God is the creator of all things and that the human being has the creative capacity granted by God from the moment he gives him the order and ability to procreate. The human being is an intelligent being. We are created equal in value but different in function and purpose. Therefore, everything that is indicated above, which we totally believe, should make you think and feel that we are genuinely like God in many things. Let us meditate deeply on this. Unfortunately, there are people who think that health consists of not having physical problems and that their spirituality is decisive for having true health (equilibrium).

For these purposes, let us clarify this matter. It is very important for us to be correct and very clear. It is necessary to know how the human being is formed, since there is a lot of confusion regarding man's true identity, and to understand the nature of the human being. The Bible says about man's origin in Genesis 2:7 that man, being a living being, is an indivisible unit and is a biopsychosocial-spiritual unit in which there is mutual interdependence between each of its faculties. It means that it is a biological, social, and spiritual entity and is also a psychological being. In other words, there are four faculties of the human being—mental faculties, spiritual faculties, physical faculties, and social faculties—which are interconnected and do not develop independently. This means that everything you do to develop your mental faculties will affect the development of your social, spiritual, and physical faculties. There can be no physical development without affecting the other areas of life. The breath of life that God gives is the power that God grants to human beings to live. The breath of life without a physical body cannot generate life.

The Bible to refer to the living being uses the phrase *nephesh hayah*. This phrase is composed of two words. The word *nephesh* means, "soul, living being, person, life," and this phrase is translated as a living being or as a living soul. This leads us to the conclusion that the soul is a living being and not an immaterial entity, in which the soul can die. The word *soul* refers to a person like all of us, not having a soul but as a soul. That is why we emphasize that man is a person, a living being, and a soul that has life. So if the soul can die, it can also get sick, hurt, and saddened because it feels and suffers. This also means that if these things can happen to the soul, health does not necessarily have to consist of (whether or not) having physical problems and that your spirituality is decisive to have true health or balance.

On the other hand, we would like to address an issue that seems somewhat conflictive to us, but in order to help those people who have sexual-identity problems, we would like to help them understand the proper use of their sexuality. In such a case, we want to explain to these people that the Bible makes clear the definition of the sexes and sexuality for the welfare of society and that sexuality and its manifestation were given before the entry of sin into humanity. The Bible also tells us that God created the human race and two sexes, male and female, with no option to another kind of sex. Both are equal before God, each with their own characteristics that define them as such. None is greater than the other, and any other (sexual option) is a deformation of sexuality as a product of sin.

Science helps us define what is sex and what is sexuality, and the factors that determine sex are the cells in the woman's body that contain two X chromosomes (XX), which, in women, we can see the creative activity of God using its ability to gestate and bring life to the world. While the cells in the man's body have an X and a Y chromosome (XY), which explains that the male does not have the same attribute as the female. But nevertheless, we see that, in the male, the physical strength and its capacity to give physical protection is, in general, much greater than in the female.

That is why we see how God, when he created us, made us equal in value but with clear differences in terms of our sexuality. It is because of these differences that it is natural for a man to feel the need for a woman and vice versa. But this manifestation of sexuality must be carried out according to God's plans; otherwise, it will lead to unhappiness. Do you know who is the primary cause? The first cause was the beginning of all things. The first cause is God, and being God from all eternity, he determined to form the universe for his own lofty and worthy ends. This is why the universe began to exist, by a voluntary act of an infinite and eternal person. He did not make things out of existing matter but made everything out of nothing, according to his own infinite wisdom. The creation of the world was not an arbitrary act but was in accordance with the infinite goodness and wisdom of the Creator. God, in his infinite wisdom, has planned all things from the beginning and causes them to happen according to his eternal purpose and at the right time.

We are convinced that the universe was created for the glory of God and not for purposes that could please us. We believe that this explains that God is the first cause and why that first cause was the beginning of all things. God's providence is his holiest, wisest, and most powerful work by which he preserves and governs his creatures and their actions.

We would like to give you, according to our opinion, what was Eve's mistake that led her to disobedience. Eve, having this encounter with the snake, her curiosity awoke, and instead of fleeing from that place to meet her husband, perhaps at least to ask him about the snake that was speaking to her, she stayed there listening to it. In other words, instead of running away, she began to discuss with it. This was Eve's mistake that led her to disobedience, which, with this attitude assumed by her, also resulted in the fall of Adam.

As a result of this fall of the first couple, we know that human nature was degraded because of sin—which, with this reality, meant that, as a consequence, man was lost—and that the world created by God would be filled with mortals condemned to misery, sickness, and death and that there was no way of escape for the offender. In this situation, this means the acceptance that we, too, are offenders exposed to suffer the consequences of sin, and in the face of this reality, we must understand that the best we can do, without a doubt, is draw closer to God in a constant concern and search for our salvation.

At some point, someone could ask you this question or something similar: If the human being was made in the image of God but then the nature of man was degraded by sin, do you believe that the human being is totally free? It is clear that the human being was made in the image of God and that he was made as a biopsychosocial-spiritual being and that it is impossible to separate these dimensions. But that sin affected them all, since it affected the totality of being not only its spiritual dimension but also its mental dimensions and its ability to socialize and, of course, its physical part.

Therefore, all this makes us think that the human being is not totally free. We believe it this way because the human being, before his fall, was perfect and did not know sin. But by disobeying, he lost communion with God. The real problem is not in the actions of sin but in our state of separation from God. There are people, and it is unfortunate, who ask themselves this following question: Can we argue that although God does not know what the people he has created are going to do, with all that, he can continue to rule the rest of the universe in an orderly way?

Within the eternal purpose of God, nothing happens that does not fit into this eternal plan. He made everything and rules everything, and everything is included in his eternal purpose. The Bible makes no exceptions when it speaks of God's rule over the world. According to the Bible, God governs everything and is very clear in this regard. Theology is in perfect harmony with the Bible when it affirms that, for that eternal purpose, God has foreordained everything that happens and that everything is totally in command of the creator.

Therefore, we cannot maintain that God does not know what the people he has created can do, much less cannot continue to rule the universe in an orderly way. We also want to take advantage of this current of thought to introduce another question that also circulate in the air in many places, and these are the questions: Since when does the idea of the immorality of the soul exist? Who was the author of this idea, and what are their aims? The idea of the immorality of the soul exists since Eve's encounter with the serpent, where Satan made, with subtlety and his lies, Eve and consequently Adam also sin. Satan was the author of this idea, and his aims were to first deceive Eve and then use it to make Adam fall. And the idea of the immorality of the soul continued from generation to generation, as we have been able to notice that it has reached our days.

For these reasons already presented, those of us who serve Christ in spirit and in truth must be more than well prepared to present the plan of salvation to a person who is puzzled or afflicted by some universal conflict that person could be experiencing in the present

world. At this time and under those circumstances, it is quite difficult, though not impossible, to present the plan of salvation to such
a person. But no matter what situation you are facing, our duty is to
tell you about Jesus Christ as the only alternative to your problem.

One of the things that must be explained is that we are part of
the largest and oldest conflict that has existed in the universe, which
is the war between good and evil. But as in every war, there are tears
and blood. Tears and blood are shed for Jesus. People need to know
that the battlefield is in the mind and in the heart. Let them also
know that every day and every moment, we are under heavy bom-
bardment without respite. But we are not alone. Jesus is with us to
fight against any conflict.

Certainly, we must explain in great detail the plan of salvation
and also invite them to accept Christ as their savior. Let us culmi-
nate this part with what the second epistle of Saint Paul says to the
Corinthians 5:21: "God made him who had no sin to be sin for us, so
that in him we might become the righteousness of God." This should
make us feel grateful to God for having saved us in an undeserved
and gratuitous way, since Christ, without deserving death, died for
us, becoming sin in our place.

Understanding the plan of salvation that God used for us and
through Jesus Christ makes us feel guilty about his death and repentant and afraid to sin. God made Christ into sin so that we might be
made the righteous of God in him. Christ exchanges his righteousness for our sin so that we can be just and not sinful. And what we
should receive as payment for our sin (death), Jesus received for us so
that we may have salvation.

We can do the right thing, but only when we accept his righteousness in exchange for our sins does our spiritual life begin. But
this does not stop here. Let us continue acquiring more knowledge.
From principle, it would seem that if God created all things, then evil
must have been created by God. However, here we have an assump-
tion that needs to be clarified. Evil is not a "thing" like a rock or
electricity. You can't have a jug of evil! Rather, evil is something that
happens, like running.

Evil does not exist by itself; it really is the lack of a good thing. For example, holes are real, but they only exist in something else. We call a hole the lack of earth, but it cannot be separated from the earth. When God made creation, it is true that everything that existed was good. One of the good things that God made was creatures with the freedom to choose the good. To make a real choice, God had to allow more than good to choose. So God sent these free beings, both angels and humans, to choose between good and the absence of it (evil). When there is a bad relationship between two good things, we call it evil, but that does not make it a "thing" that required God's creation.

Maybe the following illustration will help us: If I asked an ordinary person, "Does cold exist?" Their answer would be yes. However, this is incorrect. Cold does not exist. Cold is the absence of heat. Similarly, darkness does not exist. This is the consequence of the lack of light. Similarly, evil is the absence of good, or rather, evil is the absence of God.

God did not create evil but rather only allowed the absence of good. Let's look at the example of Job in chapters 1 and 2 of the book of Job. Satan wanted to destroy Job, and God allowed Satan to do whatever he wanted, except kill Job. God allowed this to happen to prove to Satan that Job was righteous, because he loved God and not because God had blessed him greatly.

God is sovereign and has absolute control of whatever happens. Satan cannot do anything without the "permission" of God. God did not create evil, but he allows it. If God did not allow the possibility of evil, both angels and humans would serve God by obligation and not by choice. God did not want to create "robots" that would simply do what he wanted them to do through their "programming." God allowed the possibility of evil so that we can genuinely have the freedom to choose whether or not we want to serve him.

Conclusively, there is no answer to these questions that we can fully understand. We, as finite human beings, can never understand an infinite God (Romans 11:33–34). Sometimes we think we understand why God is doing something, only to find out later that it was for different purposes than we originally thought. God sees things from an eternal perspective. We look at things from an earthly perspective.

Why did God put man on earth, knowing that Adam and Eve would sin and bring evil, death, and suffering to the entire human race? Why didn't he just create us and leave us in heaven where we would be perfect and have no suffering? The best answer we can think of is that God did not want a race of robots without free will. God had to allow the possibility of evil for us to make a true decision to worship God or not. If we had never suffered and experienced evil, would we really appreciate how wonderful heaven is? God did not create evil, but he allows it. If he had not allowed it, we would be worshipping God out of obligation and not out of the free choice of our will. It is a great privilege, which we have every day, to seek God through his divine word! Knowing Christ, through the holy word, is loving God and all things related to him.

CONCLUSION

We hope that all our readers are already sure of the significance and what it means that Jesus died for our sins, because it is good that we are very clear about this, since, without the death of Jesus through crucifixion because of our sins, no one would have eternal life. Jesus himself said, "I am the way, and the truth, and the life; no one comes to the father except through me" (John 14:6). Through this clear statement, Jesus gives us the reason for his birth, death, and resurrection to allow us the precious opportunity of the way to heaven, especially for a sinful humanity, who could never have reached heaven on their own.

Let us remember again that when God created Adam and Eve (who were the first couple of creation), they were perfect in every sense of the word and literally lived in a paradise, as we have previously mentioned, on the garden of Eden (Genesis 2:15). We have also mentioned that God created us in his image and in his likeness, which means that we also had the freedom to make decisions and choose on our own.

Genesis 3 describes how Adam and Eve succumbed to Satan's temptations and lies. In doing so, they disobeyed God's will to increase their intellect by eating from the tree of knowledge from which they had been forbidden: "And the Lord God commanded the man, 'You are free to eat from any tree in the garden; but you must not eat from the tree of the knowledge of good and evil, for when you eat from it you will certainly die.'" (Genesis 2:16–17). Indeed, this was the first sin. By virtue of our sinful nature inherited from Adam, God declared that all who sin would die, both physically and spiritually. This is the destiny of all humanity. But God, in his grace and mercy, provided a solution to this dilemma and allowed his son to shed his blood on the cross for us all. God declared that "without the shedding of blood there is no remission of sins" (Hebrews 9:22), but the remission is provided through the shedding of blood.

The law of Moses (Exodus 20:2–17) provided a way for people to be considered "sinless" or "just" in God's eyes—the offering of animals sacrificed for sin. These sacrifices were only temporary. Although, they really were a foreshadowing of what would be perfect, of the sacrifice of Christ on the cross, done once, and we are forever more than sure of this carefully compiled material on a completely theological level (Hebrews 10:10).

For this powerful reason, it was why Jesus came and why he died to become the last and final sacrifice, the perfect sacrifice for our sins (Colossians 1:22; 1 Peter 1:19). Through him, the promise of eternal life with God becomes effective through the faith of those who believe in Jesus "so that what was promised, being given through faith in Jesus Christ, might be given to those who believe" (Galatians 3:22). These two words, *faith* and *believe*, are crucial to our salvation. It is through believing in the blood of Christ shed for our sins that we receive eternal life. "For it is by grace you have been saved, through faith—and this is not from yourselves, it is the gift of God—not by works, so that no one can boast" (Ephesians 2:8–9).

Now let us briefly explain, before concluding, what it means or what the story is. History has been a true story, which has been narrated or written, of certain important events or past events that have stood out through time. These stories can very well refer to famous people, transcendental cultures, people, languages, or nations. History is cataloged worldwide as a science.

History can benefit in many ways, since the knowledge of it extends to know events and origins of the past. This knowledge can very well help us increase intelligence and the easy handling of the issues in question. On the other hand, history benefits us because by being able to have access to certain many past events that we can learn from writings, they can very easily shed light on mistakes that have been made. When we become aware of them, it gives us the opportunity not to repeat them and even so much more, perhaps even to regret them.

Concerning the death of the apostle Peter, it is clear from history that he was crucified head down on an X-shaped cross in Rome, in fulfillment of Jesus's prophecy (John 21:18). The following are the most popular reports regarding the death of other apostles. Matthew suffered martyrdom in Ethiopia, having died from a sword wound. John faced martyrdom when he was cooked in a huge cauldron of boiling oil during a wave of persecution in Rome. However, he was miraculously spared from death. Then he was sentenced to the mines in the prison of the Island of Patmos, and it was there that he wrote his prophetic book of Revelation. Later, the apostle John was released and taken back to what we know today as Turkey. He died very old and was the only one of the apostles who died peacefully.

James, the brother of Jesus (not having been officially an apostle), was the leader of the church in Jerusalem. He was thrown from a height of more than one hundred feet from the southeast pinnacle of the temple, when he refused to deny his faith in Christ. When they discovered that he survived the fall, his enemies beat him with a club to death. This was the same pinnacle where Satan is believed to have led Jesus during the temptation.

They can also guide us better in relation to our current behavior. Therefore, knowing the history of any matter in this regard is beneficial to us in one way or another. We ask ourselves, How do we relate faith to history? Especially not having been part of history and not having been an eyewitness, but through writing, do we come to take for granted what we study and accept it by faith?

By the way, in relation to what we have been presenting, a good example would be the following: We ask, Does the Bible record the death of the apostles? How did each of the apostles die? The only death of the apostles recorded in the Bible is that of James (Acts 12:2). King Herod killed James "with the sword," probably a reference to the beheading. The circumstances of the death of the other apostles can only be known based on information collected by scholars of the historical writings that have been reached.

Bartholomew, also known as Nathanael, was a missionary in Asia. He testified in what is now Turkey and was martyred for his preaching in Armenia, where he was whipped to death. Andrew was crucified on an X-shaped cross in Greece. After being severely beaten by seven soldiers, they tied his body to the cross with ropes to prolong his agony. His followers reported that when he was carried to the cross, Andrew greeted it with these words: "I have long wanted and waited for this happy moment." He continued to preach to his executioners for two days until he died.

The apostle Thomas was pierced with a spear in India during one of his missionary trips to establish a church there. Matthias—the apostle chosen to replace Judas Iscariot, the traitor—was stoned and later beheaded. The apostle Paul was tortured and later beheaded by the vile Roman Emperor Nero in the year 67. There is also information referring to the other apostles, but unfortunately none that has a historical basis or reliable data.

How the apostles died is not so important. What is important is the fact that all of them were willing to die for their faith. If Jesus had not risen, the disciples would have known it. People will not die for something they know to be a lie. The fact that all the apostles were willing to die horrible deaths, refusing to renounce their faith in Christ, is tremendous evidence that they actually witnessed the resurrection of Jesus Christ. This becomes a relationship where history was agreed with faith.

We hope, and it is our deep wish, that all this information compiled here can serve our readers with much blessing and with a wide and clear knowledge of those matters related to the crucifixion, which we have tried to enclose in this book *The Hidden Reality Surrounding the Environment of the Crucifixion of Jesus Christ*. It is a book that is born from the thesis that was elaborated in compliance with the great commission that has been given to us by God in favor of all people without any discrimination regarding race, nations, language, or gender, in consideration and respect for the authorities of the places where this book can reach. Amen.

ETYMOLOGY

Terms and Definitions

The following terms and definitions are properly defined and confirmed with reliable sources:

1. *Word of wisdom.* It is the revelation of a deed that must take place at a given time.
2. *Word of knowledge.* It is the revelation of a deed that has already occurred (a lie told by someone; a robbery committed).
3. *Discernment of spirits.* It is the revelation of the presence of evil spirits in someone or over someone or in some place.

To this end, when the Lord, in a dream or vision or by an audible voice, predicts a special event, we are faced with the revelation of the word of wisdom. When the Lord reveals in a dream or a vision or by an audible voice something that has already happened, we have the revelation of a word of knowledge. And when the Lord makes us see in a dream or vision the evil spirits doing some bad works or are ready to do it, we are faced with the discernment of the spirits.

In relation to the dreams, visions, and revelations written in the Bible that the ancients previously experienced and that were useful for them, without a doubt, will also be useful for those to whom they are given today, according to the will of God.

Dreams, visions, and revelations

Let's move on to explain what a dream is, then what a vision is, and what constitutes a revelation. Holy Scripture teaches that God speaks to man also through dreams, visions, and an audible voice. In fact, the Bible contains many dreams and visions given by God to many in ancient times as well as many cases in which God spoke, making his voice be heard. A divine dream is a dream that God gives to man under certain circumstances while he is sleeping. There are no waking dreams. Every human being dreams when he sleeps, and among the dreams, there may be some that are of God. This is true in the case of both believers and unbelievers. Now let's consider some biblical examples of dreams revealed in the Bible:

1. God came to King Abimelech at night in a dream to tell him that the woman he had taken, who is Sarah, had a husband. Therefore, he should restore her, and if he had not done so, he would have died with his whole house (see Genesis 20:1–7).
2. Jacob had a dream in which he saw a stairway. Its start is resting on the ground, its end touched the sky, and angels went up and down it. And God spoke to him (see Genesis 28:10–22).
3. While Jacob was serving Laban, he had a dream in which God showed him how he had seen everything Laban did to him and ordered him to return to his land (see Genesis 31:10–13).
4. God came to Laban in a dream, while he was chasing Jacob, and told him not to speak to Jacob either good or bad (see Genesis 31:22–25).
5. Joseph, son of Jacob, had dreams in which God predicted that his brothers would, one day, bow down before him (see Genesis 37:5–11).
6. While Joseph was in prison in Egypt, the chief butler and the chief of the bakers, who had been put in prison for a

wrong done to Pharaoh, both received in the same night a dream, one by one, in which God predicted what would happen to them after three days. These dreams were interpreted by Joseph, and things happened according to his interpretation (see Genesis 40:1–22).

7. Pharaoh, while Joseph was in prison, had two dreams in which God predicted seven years of plenty and seven years of famine. In this case, too, the dreams were interpreted by Joseph, who was released from prison by Pharaoh to interpret these dreams (see Genesis 41:1–36).

8. King Solomon had a dream in which God appeared to him and asked him to ask him what he wanted, and Solomon asked for a wise heart (see 1 Kings 3:4).

9. Joseph, Mary's husband, had a dream just when he was about to secretly leave Mary (because she was pregnant), and in this dream, an angel of the Lord appeared to him and told him not to worry about taking Mary as his wife (see Matthew 1:18–25).

10. Some wise men from the East, after finding and worshipping the baby Jesus, received a dream in which God told them not to return to Herod (see Matthew 2:12).

All these dreams and these visions were interpreted, and their interpretations turned out true. But you have to be careful with all the people who only tell you about false dreams, false visions, and revelations and who never speak about the true things, because there are false manifestations that exist. But if there are false things, there are also true things that cannot be done wrong, and the latter must be sought.

In saying this, we reiterate that scripture cannot be broken by any dream, vision, or revelation, and that it remains always, everywhere, and in any case the final authority in matters of doctrine and conduct. We always have to refer to the Bible. It must always be examined to see if the things that are said are true. So with all these dreams, visions, and revelations, we must be careful; we must not embrace them if we do not have to vigorously refute them.

Visions

The vision is a divine manifestation in which God suddenly makes us see and sometimes even hear things. The visions can be at night and during the day, that is, they can occur both at night and during the day. Not only that, they can be received with both eyes open and eyes closed. Visions written in the Bible are much more numerous than dreams. Let's mention just a few:

1. Abraham received a vision in which God spoke to him and told him that his reward would be exceedingly great (see Genesis 15:1–3).
2. Moses had a vision at Horeb when the angel of the Lord appeared to him and sent him to Egypt to deliver the people of Israel (see Exodus 3:1–22).
3. The prophet Isaiah saw the Lord of Hosts seated on a high throne and high above were seraphim, and God spoke with him and sent him to prophesize to his people (see Isaiah 6:1–13).
4. The prophet Ezekiel had heavenly visions in which he saw, among other things, the cherubim and God who was sitting on a throne above them and in which God spoke to him and sent him to prophesy against his people. In some of these visions, God also showed him the many abominable works that many, in the midst of his people, were doing (see Ezekiel 1–8).
5. Daniel had several visions in which God predicted future events (see Daniel 7–10).
6. Peter, James, and John, while on the holy mountain, received a heavenly vision in which they saw Moses and Elijah talking with Jesus who was transfigured before them, and they also heard a voice from heaven (see Matthew 17:1–13).
7. While Jesus was praying in Gethsemane, he had a vision of a holy angel who appeared to comfort him (see Luke 22:43).

8. Zechariah, the father of John the Baptist, had a vision while in the temple. In this vision, an angel of God foretold John's birth (see Luke 1:5–22).
9. Mary, while betrothed to Joseph, had a vision in which the angel Gabriel appeared to her and foretold that she would give birth to a son who would be called the Son of the Most High (see Luke 1:26–38).

Note

Betrothal means that a couple was getting married that day. And at the end of that event on that day, she left for her house and he for his, and thus they were separated for a period of one year and one day. Then as this time of a year and a day passed—called this period of separation "time of betrothal"—they proceeded to come together to lead a life as a married couple. This means that when Joseph and Mary got together, they were already married. Therefore, when Joseph found that she was pregnant, and since he loved her very much, he did not want to defame her and preferred to abandon her, because he knew that they would surely kill her with stones. But when he was going away, an angel told him, "Joseph, do not be afraid to receive Mary your wife, because what is in her is the work of the Holy Spirit."

10. The women who had gone to the tomb to anoint Jesus had a vision of angels, who told them that Jesus had risen from the dead (see Matthew 28:1–7; Mark 16:1–7; Luke 24:1–12).
11. Saul of Tarsus, named Paul, on his way to Damascus to arrest the saints and bring them in chains to Jerusalem, had a heavenly vision in which Jesus Christ appeared to him and spoke to him, establishing him as his minister (see Acts 9:1–6).
12. Paul, while he was blind in Damascus, while praying, saw in a vision a man named Ananias, who would enter the

house where he was and lay his hands on him to restore his sight (see Acts 9:10–16).

The revelations

Revelation is the manifestation by which God makes known to men truths that they would be incapable of knowing by themselves. Revelation literally means to remove the veil that hides something. God has revealed himself; he has spoken so that we may know him. And the only reason has been his love for us, wanting to share with us his divine and Trinitarian nature. Only by knowing and believing in Sacred Scripture as divine revelation do we have a true meaning in our biblical reading, and only then will we be able to listen with faith to the message that God wants to say to each one of us.

Some biblical examples are those of the prophet Elijah when, while he was in Horeb, the voice of God came to him and said, "What are you doing here, Elijah?" (1 Kings 19:13), to which he responded. And later he went on to tell him to go to Damascus to anoint Hazael as king of Syria, Jehu as king of Israel, and Elisha as prophet in his place (see 1 Kings 19:15–18).

Another example is that of the ancient prophet in Bethel who, with a lie, had brought back a man of God (making him disobey God) and that while he was eating at the table with the latter, God spoke to him and predicted his judgment against the man of God who had returned (See 1 Kings 13:20–22). This manifestation was also very present in the life of Moses, to whom God spoke his word many times, as a man speaks with another man. Stephen said that Moses received words of life to give to us (Acts 7:38). The evangelist Philip had a revelation while on the highway that leads from Jerusalem to Gaza. When he saw the eunuch in his chariot, at that moment, the Spirit said to him, "Go to that chariot and stay near it" (Acts 8:29).

The apostle Peter had a revelation after having received that vision in ecstasy at Joppa, where he saw something like a great canvas descending from heaven in which there were all the terrestrial quadrupeds and reptiles and birds of the sky. And a voice came to him: "Get up, Peter, kill and eat," and at his rejection, the voice told him not to call what God cleansed common (Acts 13:2).

Lastly, I want to tell you that we, the children of God, to understand God's will for us, should not always wait for a dream or a vision or a revelation because God has not decreed to direct us exclusively in this way. Certainly, in some cases, God will reveal certain things in this way, but in other cases, he will guide us through Holy Scripture, which is a lamp to our feet and a light to our paths. What the word of God commands us, we must do without question and without asking for a particular revelation.

We conclude that the Bible is not merely a human book, but that there is a higher value in it, as it is inspired by God and is a revealed truth of faith. It is very disturbing when this desire does not exist in a believer. I hope you understand that every word of wisdom and knowledge is helpful, and through them, God is exalted and feared. Therefore, it is necessary for a believer to want to receive dreams, visions from heaven, and divine revelations.

Gallows, from the Latin *patibulum*, is a structure raised above the ground and formed by planks where certain executions of those sentenced to death are carried out. Deuteronomy 21:22 states, "If anyone has committed a crime worthy of death, and you put him to death and hang him on a tree, you will not let his body spend the night on the tree; without fail you will bury him the same day, because cursed by God is the hanged one; and you shall not pollute your land which Jehovah your God is giving you as an inheritance." The Council of the Sanedrín, made up of seventy priests and scribes and a high priest, demanded that Pilate execute Jesus.

The gospel, meaning "good news," is better defined as the message of forgiveness of sins.

Note

To finish this part of etymology, let's read what Exodus 6:20 says: "And Amram took Jochebed, his aunt as a wife, and she gave birth to Aaron and Moses. And the years of the life of Amram were one hundred and thirty-seven years." Note that here it says that Amram, the father of Aaron and Moses, took his mother to wife and that her name was Jochebed. In other words, the mother of Aaron and Moses was the wife and aunt of their father.

ABOUT THE AUTHOR

Agustín Pimentel was born in the town of Fajardo on the beautiful island of Puerto Rico on February 18, 1943, at 2:00 p.m. At an early age, he met the Lord as he attended a church with some neighbors. Since then, he continued seeking God from the Hato Tejas neighborhood of Bayamon, but at the age of fourteen, he accepted Jesus Christ as his Savior. He studied and obtained a diploma in social sciences with a specialization in political science at the University of Puerto Rico.

In his career, he dedicated himself to evangelization and the pastorate inside and outside of Puerto Rico. By 1991, he moved to Philadelphia to continue evangelizing and presided over the Agua De Vida Evangelistic Movement, an incorporation which God had placed in his hands to preside over since July 6, 1978. He was working as a social worker for ten years at the Associated Services For the Blind, an organization that offers services to blind people, and also around ten years, he worked as an announcer on Radio Salvación, a radio station in Philadelphia. He was not counting the years that he was working in secular jobs, such as in Puerto Rico, as a heavy-truck driver; in the Puerto Rico Land Authority, as a seller of automotive parts; in the United States, as a turner mechanic; and not to mention a long history as a radio programmer in different radio stations from the Dominican Republic, Puerto Rico, and the United States. It was in Philadelphia where he began his university studies with Dayspring

Theological University, pursuing to concentrate more in theology. As a university student, and by the will of God, he attained a master's in theology and also a doctorate in theology. And by the grace of God, he has been able to finish a PhD doctoral specialty in theology.

This is just part of the trajectory of this author who, at the age of eighteen, went blind, but this was not an impediment that he could not overcome himself and achieve so many things with the help of God.